About the Author

Thomas Rowan is a father of three and lives in Wisconsin serving in the Air National Guard. Apart from reading and writing, Thomas spends most of his free time on various hobbies including painting, fitness, and Martial Arts.

Poems, Sonnets and Short Stories

Thomas Rowan

Poems, Sonnets and Short Stories

Olympia Publishers
London

www.olympiapublishers.com
OLYMPIA PAPERBACK EDITION

Copyright © Thomas Rowan 2023

The right of Thomas Rowan to be identified as author of this work has been asserted in accordance with sections 77 and 78 of the Copyright, Designs and Patents Act 1988.

All Rights Reserved

No reproduction, copy or transmission of this publication may be made without written permission. No paragraph of this publication may be reproduced, copied or transmitted save with the written permission of the publisher, or in accordance with the provisions of the Copyright Act 1956 (as amended).

Any person who commits any unauthorised act in relation to this publication may be liable to criminal prosecution and civil claims for damage.

A CIP catalogue record for this title is available from the British Library.

ISBN: 978-1-80439-380-2

This is a work of fiction. Names, characters, places and incidents originate from the writer's imagination. Any resemblance to actual persons, living or dead, is purely coincidental.

First Published in 2023

Olympia Publishers
Tallis House
2 Tallis Street
London
EC4Y 0AB

Printed in Great Britain

Dedication

This book is dedicated to my parents, Shane and Kristina Rowan.

Poems, Sonnets and Short Stories

Poetry

Love Comes Softly

When once in my loneness did bound,
The sea of thoughts racing around,
Time suddenly stood still, as if controlled by another force with skill.
At first I couldn't render the reason,
My thoughts scrambled without cohesion,
It took some time but then I knew,
That my heart was wrestling with feelings for you.
With eyes so blue they sparkled like the sea,
My heart jumped each time she looked at me.
Her touch so gentle and full of compassion,
A touch that fills me with passion.
Each time I see her, I can't help but wonder,
Why she pulls my heart asunder.
It shouldn't be this way, she's not mine to have,
And she cannot stay.
It became a feeling that I didn't expect to obtain.
From one yet, I fear I must abstain.
For the one who my heart does yearn,
Belongs to another and I must retain,
Though it hurts to put myself in this strain,
My heart still fights against the grain.
My desire is to her and everything,
Despite the constant pain and sting.
She doesn't realize how deep her words go,

From which my heart and feelings flow,
My mind is drunk and full of fear,
For each day apart causes my heart to sear.
I couldn't stop this feeling,
For I didn't know it was coming,
Until it was overwhelming,
The beat of my heart ever harder drumming.
It's too late now, and I must accept it,
To myself I must admit,
That this love of mine is not able to be met,
Perhaps it's best I just forget.
And yet here it is, though it shouldn't be,
Sometimes you can't control it, when love, comes softly.

Silence

I am too tired to speak, this wooden bench my only friend.
A day outside to brighten the mood,
And this old soul to mend.
This life of mine had got to me, so here I sit in silence.
The birds that flutter while around,
Give to me a strange alliance.

I haven't much left to care for, for all my friends are gone.
For you see, I've been sitting here since the nearly dawn.
I suppose I should get up and go, and my life to live,
So sorry if I bother you, my attitude please forgive.

But if you struggle too, you are welcome to share,
This old wooden bench and ponder life's tedious affair.
Sometimes you just need someone, to sit with you in peace.
I think you'll find a new view on life and enjoy the sweet release.

So, if you feel too tired to speak,
In search of internal guidance,
Please, sit next to me,
For I too, am fluent in silence.

You

Questions that pry into my mind,
As my feelings start to define.
What it is that I am dreaming?
With all the thoughts inside me teeming.
Thoughts connect to feelings so deep,
I lie here again losing sleep.
The drum beating within my chest,
Does steal away again my rest.

It is no mystery to me, for I know why the feelings plea,
Plea to myself and inside me muster,
Each time enough to cause a fluster.
Though I do not fight it, like some others might do,
For when my heart gets like this,
I know it's because of you.

Do you love me, like I love you?
For I know when love is true,
How else can I explain what I feel?
These wounds that refuse to heal.
The feelings that tear my heart asunder,
Enough to make any man shudder.
To me instead brings a painful bliss,
One I would not have desist.

Instead rather, I would pursue,
For I know, they are because of you.
Feelings that though they be heavy,
I know them too well already.
These feelings it would seem, nestled deep and in between,
Are always there, and never seen.

Hey God, Me Again

Hey God, me again, I hope that I do not cry to you in vain,
I know I should not worry,
As all creation tells of your glory,
For you are good, and perfect, true and holy,
Unchanging as the Bible story.
But I feel I am not good enough,
To even ask, nor plead for stuff.

But the stuff I seek isn't careless items,
Nor meaningless vices,
Gone are the wishes of youthful thoughts
and pointless surprises.
For now my requests are more inwardly driven,
And I seek again to be forgiven.
But beyond that, I seek the strength,
And to be encompassed in your love's embrace.

So here I am, once again on my knees,
Wishing I didn't need words like these.
I know that you hear me, I know you're there,
And even so, I – just humble and bare.
The cycle continues, the pain still lingers and desperately I
cling to the tips of your fingers.
A piece of your glory, a taste of forgiveness,
Longing to be rid of my sickness.

What is your answer? And when will I see it?
The freedom from this lonely pit.
Give me strength and grant me courage,
a bit to my heart encourage.
I want to do better, I know that I should,
If only my flesh and body could.
So here I beg, and here I cry,
Waiting patiently for some reply.

How many times can I come before you?
When already you know all that I'll do.
The tears fall from my face, it hurts inside,
I must be a disgrace.
How quickly each time I hide from your face,
Yet again, you show me grace.
The spirit is willing and the body, weak...
More strength from you is all I seek.

For I am afraid that as soon as I rise,
My sin will consume me again with its lies.
I know that this life you have given to me,
And for your glory and purpose be,
But I can't help but wonder, and death I ponder...
To you have my soul sent,
And here then I can be at rest,
No longer struggling under this torment.

My mission isn't over, and here I yet live under grace,
To be the reflection of your face,
Strength here now I have and then some,

Forward I go, more like you I become.
One day I will be free of my transgression,
One day I will sit in Heaven.
I am still your possession,
And all my sin is completely forgiven.

Still, I yearn for the day when I no longer struggle,
Nor under the weight of sin, buckle.
To no longer need to make amends, need no longer say,

"Hey God, me again."

Conscience

It was a cold, and windy night, sitting under the fire light.
I remember the sight,
As the flames licked the wood and the air,
Caught in the trance and in a sullen stare,
The reflection glistened in my eyes.
The shadows that it spread across the floor,
Resembled ghostly cries.

In my thoughts, as I sat there, I was drawn ever deeper,
No rest was found in my eyes, though sleep now I'd prefer,
I jumped in my skin
at the sound of the pounding in the room,
It echoed throughout the place,
As if it signaled impending doom.

The pounding continued relentlessly,
Disturbed my peace successfully,
Who is it that comes at this hour?
That takes away my thoughts so effortlessly?
I rose to answer, this riddle to solve,
Here, this situation resolve.
I opened the door and into the dark,
I peered ever further to see my mark.

No one was there, save only the dark,

Dogs, in the distance, bark,
My body grew tense, and I shut the door,
Trying in my head to make sense,
Sense of what just happened to me,
Since out the door nothing I see.
The pounding again was heard by me,
In anger I called out, "let me be".

I opened the door, nothing again was seen,
Thick blackness with a hazing sheen,
Shutting the door in disgust, and in myself losing trust.
I returned to the fireplace,
It danced and glowed with a beauty and grace,
The trust in myself was waning away,
Soon to be gone without a trace.

Suddenly the place grew smaller,
Yet the fire remained ever calmer,
The calm and entrancing presence of the flame,
Seemed to be the only thing to keep me sane.
For since I heard the knocking over again,
I felt the pulsing through my veins.
Anxious I stood there, tense and firm,
For if this is the end, let it be on my terms.

Eagerly I wished it over, harder I tried to find my closure,
But the room had other thoughts instead,
Sunken in my chair filling with dread,
I focused on the fire and still no cure was found,
For within myself did it lay bound.
And there amidst the pounding sound,

Each thought within me drowned.

These instances, they steer us through life,
Whether for happiness or strife,
And we should make peace about it,
As each moment is fixed like a stone glyph.
The past comes back to haunt you,
Each of us at some point or another,
Set here for us to rediscover,
For our conscience will not – let it smother.

Child's Play

Climbing the stairs to investigate,
As the pitter patter of feet is heard no more.
Standing outside the bedroom door,
The burdens of life – my shoulders bore,
Expecting to be full of rage as I reach the top stair,
I paused and listened as I stood there.

But it was shock and awe that took me deeply,
As I watched the children play so sweetly,
And it was here that I came to realize,
In the silence of playfulness that did surprise.
I couldn't move, nor did I want to.
For here the scene hit me through.

For it was in this moment as I gazed ever further,
Instantly I saw the innocence of the children
that moved in fervor.
It was there, at the door,
As the emotions of my heart outpoured,
Long suppressed feelings,
Which I remembered in a flash of my past, now restored.

Visions of my memories came blurred,
Whilst inside my emotions stirred,
Here they played and I watched eagerly,

And listened to the conversations carefully.
Listening to the imaginations run wildly,
Expressing their adventures oh so vividly.

Through mountains and valleys, and worlds beyond,
There is no limit,
There is no place where they didn't belong,
For it did not matter what rules that should be,
Nor how we as adults can often be,
For within the child's mind, the world they see differently.

It was here that it hit me, and alas I grow sad, for I thought
that growing up, wouldn't be that bad,
But in my life that I must traverse, I realize that it is a true
blessing and a curse – to be a dad.
Lost are the dreams of my youth, when it happened, I can't
recall, a mystery for the greatest sleuth.

But here I am reminded of the dreams I once held dear,
And as my heart begins to shear,
Here it is at the end of the day,
Watching closely as my children play,
It pains me so to hear them plea,
Plea for what they cannot see,
To wish to grow up is common I know,
If only they could see the coming sorrow.

But I believe life grants us this grace,
Through all the heartache of this place,
For how would we remember such joy?
Without the smile in a child's face?

For at this age, what can we say?
When the sweetest thing in life, is simply –

Child's play.

Here I Sit in this Chair

Here I sit in this chair,
Stressed out enough to lose my hair,
My wife yells at me for so much as word,
Her voice right now though, I wish I hadn't heard.

The doctor says three more hours of walking,
She yells at me again because I'm still talking.
For better or worse I said,
Even when her face gets angry and red.

I love you and always will,
Even when you wish your looks could kill.
Her labor pains come and go,
Though my funny side I dare not show.

All jokes aside I'm sure it sucks,
When you're forced to waddle just like ducks.
All nine months she bragged the pain wouldn't be that bad,
I chuckle to myself.

But if I said, "I told you so", she might get just a little mad,
My daughter is here with head of dark brown hair,
She is so beautiful as I hold her.
Here, as I sit, in this chair.

As Love Grows

I was lonely and alone,
Wandering through this life,
Not content, while my emotions groan.
Suddenly, your presence cutting like a knife.

And in that moment my heart was gone,
To you now, did it belong.
That moment when I heard you speak,
A voice so soft, so sweet it made my soul weak.

Always constantly thinking of you,
Things we'd say, how it'd be, what we'd do.
To be together, I knew I must try,
I couldn't pass this up, the way you kept catching my eye.

I know you have past baggage,
I'm not free myself from this claim.
But through our time together
Know that my love will remain the same.

You find it hard to express your feelings,
In words, what lies beneath.
Know in your actions I find your meaning.
While you keep the sword of your words in its sheath.

Through my words and my deeds
Know that I am true.
That from the beginning you planted the seeds,

That brought me to love you.

I hope that as time goes on,
That I can be a man who.
That while you weigh the pros and cons,
That I can earn the "I Love You Too".

A Mother

Every day I work and push myself.
Wondering why I live this way.
I need not look very far though,
Each goodnight kiss, each and every birthday.
It's not something that I learned, though some help I admit I need.
I didn't feel I was ready at first.
But to the will of life, I must concede.

I have never given up, though many times I wish I could.
Interesting as it is, those thoughts would only last a moment,
For as the years go on, I start to yearn and miss each component.
It is not all bad, and to change my life I realized that I never would.

Good, bad, or indifferent. I would do it again and love this way.
I understand it's not for everyone,
And it's different, person to person.
Yet here I stand, proud in my choices,
And I will make this bold assertion –
I hold myself together, my love is strong,
And I have not given to dismay.

Still, often times we stand alone, even though it should not be,
But even when we have a partner, they will not often see.
And though my children are loved by others and their father,
My love is very different –
Because I am a mother.

Alone

It was the heat of the summer long ago, I remember oh so clearly,
As I wrestled with the thoughts about my life,
And what I cling to so dearly.
Dearly I cling to these thoughts of mine,
for no one may have them, save only time.
Time to which I am bound and yet I feel and the emotions pound,

Pound at my heart, and at my head…
I cannot tell if it be happiness or dread.
Please help me find some relief,
Relief of this feeling, and let the emotions cease.
But alas, I am lonely, and so my heart in it beating spoke only,
Only in this feeling that created this thought in me teeming.

For no one else can know my secrets, judgement is all I will find.
Judgement for what they don't understand, criticism, for my grind.
Where I come from, and where I go, is my story, and mine alone.
Alone to endure, and to work through, to my heart, let it be known.

My thoughts again attack me, I cannot fight them anymore.
Please help me find relief,
And help to find solace from the burden's bore,
To me in my loneliness, I think I have it all, but not.
This feeling in my heart has ever been present in what I've wrought.

For I sit in sadness and my thoughts,
My stomach sits in twisted knots,
My heart is heavy when it is only me,
I long to love, and with someone be.

For it is not good that man should be alone,
A truth to me that has been made known.
Because when you have a heart that cries out for support,
You instantly regret, being alone.

Dream On

Dream on my little ones,
The time is almost here.
For the world gets strange as you grow up,
But there is nothing yet to fear.

Dream on my little ones,
Each of you, your own.
Some extra time I wish I had,
Still, I can't wait to see you grown.

Dream on my little ones,
So many questions yet to ponder.
I answer what I can,
Leaving your mind, a bit to wonder.

Dream on my little ones,
There is nothing yet to fear.
For as long as my time is on this Earth,
Your daddy is always here.

Here I Sit

Here I sit, caught in guessing, why my heart again did flutter,
And still with no answer, straining to understand what it did utter.
What it means that my heart beams with such a feeling,
This feeling to me strange, as I have no way to know its meaning.

The sun's gaze through the window,
reflected off the dust and pressed,
Further it pierced into my room, attempting to light up the doom,
The doom which still hung in my head,
its answer yet I still guessed.
Continued seeking the meaning, while yet holding to it teeming.

Here I sit, focused on what I feel inside,
hearing nothing but my breathing.
The sunlight now glinting gently on the glass,
its warm rays now crossing my path,
And here I begin to wonder,
glancing back into the heart to see the aftermath.
I felt this warm feeling, though the sun was not the reason,
deep inside still beating.

In my chest I heard repeating, the gentle and continuous beating,
As if my heart was softly pleading…
Pleading to make my mind understand its meaning.
I glance further out the window near me,
and the world I see what's free.
Free like my heart longs to be, yet still beating deep within me.

Here I sit, caught in guessing why my heart again did flutter,
But now, I have my answer, and so I begin to mutter,
Speak of what my heart tries to reveal and see,
For it is love, that has pressed this feeling in me.

I Am a Father

Do I believe in love at first sight?
A question often asked to me, and I have dwelt on this thought,
An idea so simple, yet so deep; I need to be sure; I need to be right.
I thought more about the question, this thought, harder than it aught.
It bothered me, to solve this mystery, and seek the answer here.

Throughout my time I sit and wonder,
How love moves with such splendor.
The splendor of the feeling, and the emotion that is teeming,
Teeming with its different meanings… so simple yet full of grandeur.
This at first difficult to decipher,
For the words escape me and I cannot answer,
Yet this riddle to solve I must seek out further,
Have I felt this love myself I wonder?

Yes. I realize, I know the answer.
To this question that is posed to me,
For I understand the meaning now,
I look deep into love, and I can see.

For in my life there have been those that came,
And that feeling arose –
Instantly and without hesitation, as I seek to answer the question.
And now here I end my session.

For it has been made clear to me, how a love like this might just be,
For in my heart I know where it lies, and how it came to me.
And it seems that every year; it gets, and grows a little stronger,
Do I believe in love at first sight?
Of course I do, I am a father.

Long Forgotten

Lost in my thoughts, tired yet restless,
As my mind pushes to regain my senses.
I remember while I sat there, lost in empty dreams,
Reflecting on my life and how meaningless it seems.

The further I remembered, the deeper I regretted,
Regretted most if not all, of the soon forgotten lore.
Times past and memories fading, no longer safely netted,
Netted deep within my mind, lost in the tears that did outpour.

Why the tears come I wondered,
feeling in my mind the sense of rotten…
Memories that now did lose their hold, soon forgotten.
Some of love held so dear now broken –
Of thoughts that sung through one's heart that opened.

Opened wide the door, the door that in my silence,
I wished would once again give me guidance.
Smiling, here, as I remember what I felt like caught in,
Heart pulled, and mind broken, soon to be, long forgotten.

My thoughts continued as I sat there,
Reflections of my memories glare.
Glare back at me for but a moment,

As if asking me for some bestowment.

Broken minded I am, sitting here in my chair,
Contemplating my life's reason, in the musty air.
Here though I sit and wonder, what have I done to be set in?
Set in this place to which I can't control, till the memories are long forgotten.

This lore soon long forgotten, I sit and wish to hold,
Hold on to these, the memories so bold.
Regrets and love, and stories of a life past,
But what can we do when it was never designed to last?

Looking back as these memories fade,
Losing love, regret and more, as it is all grayed.
Wishing to hold on to them, crying more and even then,
Realizing that all too much, they were bound to leave me when.

When the time grows, beyond the reach of my mind,
Further back they recede, lost to me as though I am blind.
What has my life been till now? With every moment that I've boughten.
Boughten with my life's time and effort,

Now to all… long forgotten.

Love

Cherry blossoms – in the spring,
A soft sound of the birds that sing.
A warm breeze in the days of June.
Watching the morning-glories bloom.

It is the feeling of the warm sun,
The feeling of watching, kids have fun.
Newborn babies with cuddles so soft,
The morning glow of the gentle frost.

Strength of the waves crashing around,
Hard to understand as the feelings abound.
People are just people, and love is just a word,
Yet a feeling that drives one, to do the absurd.

Each day that passes by the heart yearns ever more.
Restless and eager, losing hope and grown to adore.
For it is one thing to say just simply "I love you".
Yet better when it's combined with "I love you too".

Once Upon a Time

Once upon a time – as the stories often go.
Like those stories, we travel and journey,
through hardship and trials.
To find myself I begin, seek out to search among the vile,
The vile and ghastly story of my life,
With all the actions I begin to sow.
Not understanding, still reminiscing –
Caught in the present of what I see,
Sight, hearing, touch, and smell, all my senses must agree.

The road goes on before me, and I must travel on,
Walking along in peaceful bliss, unaware I am – lost in the abyss.
Sword in hand, I defeat my foes,
Wandering on, but with victory I grow.
Grown with each and every win,
I neither look to the right, nor the left.
But instead, I look within…

Within myself, I seek to find, the means to justify my cause.
For this is my life's story, and here, I will pause.
For here I seek, to be well known, to get the world's applause.
Silence still, is all I hear, the chorus of cheer; never reaches my ear.

And so here I start to wonder, and my thoughts bring me to ponder.
Thoughts so deep, yet shallow in my sleep, as I realize that I squander.

No, awake I am. Still yet, in a dream…
The story of my life still goes,
Regardless of the resistance I throw.
It never seems to slow down, the choices I make, me, they surround.
Each step I see, brings me closer to what I still cannot guess to be.
But alas, perhaps it is best, for ignorance is bliss, and best for me.
No, I cry. It cannot be, how will I learn,
if life's meaning is kept from me?

This is no story; it is not a tale of the old days and times past…
This is my life, both past, present, and looking ahead,
Forever it is bound to end, though I cannot see it, the final date is set.
How long I have I do not know,
Forever though, I realize it won't last.
I try to learn from each mistake, and each tear that is shed.
I move to crush, and with each thrust, I defeat every threat.

Almost as if my end was near,
I glance back in the past and see all I can,
The joy, the heartache, with each year that passed,
I see across the span. Each day that flashes before my eyes.

Clear as day I see what's wrought,
All my effort and time that, to this place I have been brought.
The time that my life covers over, of love and casualty,
Each harmless civilian... Am I the hero of my story?
Or just, another villain?

Sister Dear

What do I say sister dear?
You've been gone a long time.
A cold stone is all that is here,
A little dingy and with some grime.

I have nothing left but one faint memory,
One I have cherished for so long.
While you sit in Heaven's treasury,
We carry on, holding strong.

Frozen in time your pictures hold,
A happy face, bright and bold.
And while time often softens death's blow,
I wonder what it'd be like to have seen you grow.

But there are no "what ifs" with Jesus,
This was His date.
And it really should please us,
To know He controlled your fate.

I will see you again,
There in Heaven's glory.
The thoughts of what would be said then,
Are enough to fill a story.

What do I say sister dear?
Standing by your stone.
Wishing you could hear,
But alas, I stand alone.

The Fear of Death

I will tell you a tale if I may,
Of a dream I once had, please let me say.
Of what has wrought me to dismay.
Not sure why, or how it was,
Of what I saw that fateful day…

Time it seemed, did not apply
With what I saw while in the sky.
It lives its life a slave to none.
…Save only one.
Who it was I must imply.

Here it comes, there it goes,
Hunting, hunting – Always hunting.
Forever it eats; yet is never full.
I see this now – forevermore.
I see this now, as I soar.

Time its weapon, yet you can find,
Others here, it'll release from binds.
So it goes as it pleases, through the dark and the light
Hunting, hunting – always hunting.
Always out of sight.

Its master calls and it will answer,

My heart beats as I watch, faster and faster
It moves with cunning – It has no shame.
Whatever it does, however it moves –
Strangely, carries no blame.

I knew its name, but too scared to say,
For it, I feared, would call me one day.
As I watched it move about.
I summoned my courage and drew a deep breath,
I shouted and called – to the one named 'Death'.

It paused to answer and came up to me
What is it? It asked. Turned with sharp degree,
What is your question? – Ask it quickly.
My courage now gone
I stare into it, it, staring at me.

Who is your master? Who do you serve?
I finally asked without reserve.
He faced me now, eye to eye,
His face though I could not see,
Just blackness there – as he sighed at me.

The one I serve, gives me my task,
I do what I must, no questions I ask.
For my time is limited, my job will soon end,
There will be a time,
When I no longer send –

Who is it? I asked, give me his name.
Who is it that controls death and the grave?

Death said nothing, simply hung his head.
You cannot fathom the answer.
Was all it said.

Then it started to leave,
No, I stated, tarry a bit longer.
When will I sleep in the eternity slumber?
Death responded and said you will not believe,
I am not all knowing so don't be naïve.

You will die when you your job is done.
Who knows when this is – no one.
You, I replied, hunting, hunting –
Always hunting,
You know who you're confronting.

Tell me, I beg you, tell me now.
Tell me my date, pray the master allow.
It bustled in its cloak all heavy and black,
Only the master knows, he decides your fate,
Leave me now, go back; go back.

You hide whom you serve and deny me my date,
Why this vison? Why meet my face?
A moment of silence, before he would state:
What you see is because of he,
He who holds the mighty key.

It is never expressed to me the 'Why?'
This is my task, now let me by.
My time is limited, don't you see?

The master is coming, his return is near.
And then my name you will no longer fear.

Again, I questioned – When will we know?
When can we – be free from your sorrow?
Death's only reply; you can never know.
I started to understand, as it became clear to me.
That this, I would just have to let be.

Death left me alone and continued his task,
My questions to him, I didn't dare ask.
It passes overall, glad, or depressed,
Happy or sad – It makes no distinction,
This thing we call 'Death.'

My vision ended, and with that I was awake,
My heart was heavy, and hands would shake.
I replayed the dream over and over,
Until at last I felt a peace,
Peace about it, and the fear ceased.

We live not knowing when we end,
We live in fear and often straight dread.
But Death does not choose who it calls,
It is he, he who holds the key.
The Master, the creator of all.

Death will come to us all one day,
And when it does, you will know.
It is time to reap, all that you have sown.
Knowing that your time is done.

Should bring a peace to you, to everyone.

The worry and stress of what is lost in fear
Learn to let go of all you hold dear.
Learn to be better than you were before.
We should not fear Death,
No, not any more.

The Feeling

As I lay in my bed, the darkness of the room looming,
Ever surrounding me so, still my thoughts ever zooming.
Zooming through my mind in an ever attempt to bring to light,
Sleep continued to escape me as I drifted into the night.

The night was pressing ever stronger, and I tossed in endless hunger,
A hunger for the reason,
That these thoughts of mine kept me in this season,
This season of restless things that stole my feeling,
As I grow never younger.
Each hour that passes, still I wait as I look into the masses.

The wave of thoughts that fly through my head,
I cannot stop them,
For if I could, I would, and feel my release into bed.
Sleep has ever been a dream, and reality it seems,
Continues to blur the lines that so meticulously deemed…

Deemed each its own position, one true the other false,
Yet they continue to mix in my mind,
Intertwined in an endless waltz.
I cannot separate the two, for they are forever bound true.
Because the truth is nothing more than my own perspective.

Perspective of the thoughts that chase me,
Becoming so much more effective,
And despite my best efforts, I am unable to be deflective,
I try to balance out the thoughts and remain to myself, subjective.
Perhaps if I break apart the thought, I can be more selective.

Choosing here what thought to break,
I sat up at once and chose to take,
Take the one that pierced ever deeper,
The one that held my heart like some creeper,
This thought that me surrounded, I realized what I had,
Reality then kept me grounded.
Just a feeling in this thought, nothing more,

Yet here in this feeling did my whole emotion pour,
There was no word to describe this feeling, and so this burden I bore.
A feeling in my heart, that caused my mind to stir,
Set up in my bedroom, as my thoughts began to blur.

No comfort could be found, restless in my bedsheets bound,
Bound again to my thoughts that had kept me so distressed,
At this time not thinking, as my eyes stare not blinking.
Stare into the endless night, clinging to the feeling tight.

I may never know the meaning, of this, complex feeling,
Pray for some sudden revelation, to put at ease this vexation.
To my knees I have been thrown, into this position prone,
Forever it seems this feeling, to me... Will be unknown.

The Mirror

In my room, at the table there, vacant and dusty, and very bare.
Save for one thing, which would cause me to stare.
The simple mirror, with a soft glare. It intrigued me –
my vanity mirror,
She entranced me, just, sitting there.
Often would I be caught, and stare,
Deep in the mirror sitting there.

Then one night, my lamp reflected,
off the mirror which had me enchanted.
The face I saw, in the clear reflection.
A figure there with a pale complexion.
My soul was pushed with huge vexation!
For the figure there in my mirror, as it became ever clearer.
Wasn't me, no, not my face, But a distorted monster –
Which stood in my place.

It was late, almost midnight, I was awake, and full of fright.
Afraid to look upon the mirror, my restless state, to reconsider.
I called my friends to come and render,
And rest my thoughts to complete surrender.
"Look!" I pleaded "Look in the mirror!"
"What do you see?"

"Nothing," they replied, "I only see me."
"Nothing more, let it be."
My mind went numb, I knew what I saw.
This issue I knew I couldn't withdraw.
Midnight again, that following night,
I went to my room and turned out the light.

I glanced at the mirror. And though it was dark,
The reflection was there, so very stark!
How can this be? With no light I see you.
How is this possible with a clear view?
I tried and tried to avoid the mirror,
For it continued to fill me with such terror.

No sleep in my eyes when the morning came.
Using the light from the windowpane,
I sat at the mirror and saw it again.
The face that has so filled me with dread.
The longer I stared, the more I wondered,
Why this face, to me, encumbered.

When I realized that what I saw,
Changed my ways, for at my soul it did gnaw.
For the face – that I looked upon. The true face, which was cast on.
The face of my soul deep in the mirror,
The reflection of me, it became even clearer.
The face in the mirror from which I try to hide,
Is just the face, of the demon inside.

The Rose

It was in the early spring, when I saw him walking past the station,
Slow and steady were his steps and he had some flowers in his hand.
I thought, as I saw him, and wondered his destination,
For as he walked his head hung low, and I yearned to understand.

Understand what brought him out, in this chilly air,
From whence he came I did not know, but I must ask where he goes.
For the flowers in his hand, were a colorful bundle –
around a single rose.
My curiosity now intrigued; I must stop him –
some time I hoped he'd spare.

Sir, I said rather bluntly. If you could wait just a moment here,
I implore to you good sir, what the meaning of your flowers is.
Tell me where you go, to what your destination is.
I incline my attention to you good sir, here please feed my ear.

He paused before answering, his head hung even lower,

The rose stands for the love we shared,
A chill went through his aged bones,
The flowers around the colorful shades,
Her favorites from the garden she bore.
I keep the garden every year and bring these flowers to her stone.

I add the rose as a special treat, she never got to see it bloom,
But each and every year, I bring these for her to see.
I miss her so much, but this task, closer to her it brings me.
She's gone now but yet I hope that they brighten up heaven's room.

I stood silent for a moment, before saying another word,
This man here before me, and shown what many in life don't see,
Little things like this, that may seem rather absurd,
But it is in these acts of love and kindness that help us all,
Better to be.

The Soldier

I am standing in a formation, alone and together.
My body moves on command, numb to all, even the weather.
Yet here in my mind, I am aware, but lost, distant and lonely.
Lost in my thoughts of this one thing only.

What choices were made and that my life has led me here?
Why am I away from all those I hold dear?
Time moves as I march, slow yet fast…
Each day counts down, each day, another passed.

I can't help but feel everything, yet nothing,
Each night I recall the memory, and its sting.
This feeling, becoming more of me as the days go,
My face is false, but I must suffer through,
My true face I dare not show.

For to survive, we must play the game.
Not to win, but to just keep playing the same.
It will be over soon, though now it seems forever,
One day soon, we will be together.

It will be better in the end.
And here I will not bend.
I, myself to this place did send,
To be better than I was, at the end.

Thinking of You

Brooding out my windowpane, leaned up, and against the frame,
Reflecting on all, and the life that is past,
Still, my mind is drawn, drawn to focus on,
The reflection in the glass,
I see myself – yet deeper still I gaze,
Why this happened and before I knew,
Knew what my thoughts had brought out to me.
I was already, thinking of you.

For this reason I cannot guess,
It has no real place nor common sense,
For I hardly know you, and yet, there you are, always present
in my thoughts so dense.
Deep within my thoughts so dense –
Your face appears, just quiet and sweet,
Memories of love I know that aren't mine, yet,
You are the thought to which I retreat.

Retreating to you and thoughts I have,
Soft yet reckless, it tears my soul.
Look to the fire and you will see what I feel,
My chest is heavy, pressed to the coals.
Burning and searing my emotional core,
Lost in the sense of this passion pressed,

Pressed to me, an uncontrolled flood, yet, still ever soft,
I would never have guessed.

I lay in my bed and drift off to sleep,
Yet still in my dreams you appear to me there,
I pull ever closer in my mind as I see you,
To remember that feeling, something so rare.
And in the dawn I remember, the impression left behind,
Like a morning dew,
Dew that rests so gently in my dreams,
Still I realize, in my subconscious, I was thinking of you.

Out in the distance, and so far out of reach,
I stare and wonder, almost ponder –
Life's pull against my heart. For if indeed if these feelings are real,
Then why suppress and not let wander.
Wander through the holds of my soul, and bring the subtle clues,
The many reasons that my mind, is always thinking of you.

Others here have come and gone, the void to fill, or so I try,
Pressed against these thoughts of mine,
With tension and relief, I sigh…
My heart is heavy, my soul is weak. My mind, how it moves,
Moves within myself, my thoughts to subdue; the feelings, and attempt to remove.

But like water it comes rushing,
Feelings and emotions, gentle yet firm,
And like fire it comes burning, pushing my heart, and ever

yearning.
Yearning for a chance to see, what lies beyond and push it through,
Bursting through, and reveal the reason as to why,
Why always, I am thinking of you.

Time

It is something we can't control,
Yet, we have used it, since long ago.
It is set, it is fixed, to be what we dread.
It is woven into life, an unbreakable thread.

If we try to outsmart this thing,
Often, we end up feeling its sting.
It has no feelings, nor listens to cries.
It stops for no one and takes no bribes.

It moves through us all and forever we dread,
One direction it goes, and only stops when we're dead.
Interesting it is, as we go through life,
Ups and downs, through peace and strife.

Still, it goes, forever forward,
Still, we go, forever onward.
If you waste it, it would be such a crime,
Since we are all the same, bound to time.

Unborn

Since the beginning I could comprehend, I am floating,
Seemingly it feels, forever nearly drifting.
Tight and secure, never falling,
Under water, yet never sinking.

Here, the voices, that are always heard,
My vision though, is constantly blurred.
I strain to understand the muffled distortions,
And adjust to the weird contortions.

I do not know fear,
Nor the pain of what burden you bear.
I understand not the pain of true sorrow,
And time, that I don't know I borrow.

The heart that beats,
With a sound so sweet.
Not my heart, though I know that sound,
That sound in me and out, it does surround.

Every day we play and such,
I can always, feel your touch.
I desperately hope you feel mine.
I couldn't know, I didn't see the signs.

To prove my worth, and gain some time,
I had hoped that forever, you'd be mine.
I cannot speak, nor express myself.
I have done so much, now – what else?

For it is hard to prove my value
While I'm caught up in a vacuum.
The loving soul here I hope you see,
The child you are about to kill – is me.

Sonnets

Mortality

Sonnet 1

How do I compare this life to the next one so far?
For since we do not ever reach the next
Till gone from this one, we are.
I remember as I sat there and saw her for the first time.
She was clothed in black and beautiful to look at –
from a certain angle.
For if you looked upon her, this lady here,
Both beauty and disaster did entangle,
Together these features did fill her face
and yet I was not afraid.
For I knew why I saw her and why to me she bade.
Some may think her cruel and unfair in her brutality.
But those are the ones that cannot accept the inevitable
That forever we are sealed… in our own mortality.

Creation

Sonnet 2

As I walk along the trail, I glanced around to see,
What I could under the veil,
The veil of the clouds above my head,
Brought about a solemn tone to the trail on which I tread.
'Twas here I found a flower,
And though I could not guess its power,
I pondered at the flower, stopped, and examined it closer,
Time around me moved even slower,
While I stared at this special flower.
No distraction could break my gaze,
It was if my mind was in a haze,
Forever trapped in this daze –
that kept me locked full of delays.
I neither cared for those around me,
Nor the time of my day it was,
For if no one else could see, what this flower means to me,
Then let them forever be, cast away, and forever free.
The longer that I sat there affected,
The more I felt connected.
Connected to the flower and to its maker more subjected.
For all creation sings His glory,
Our lives here, just part of the story.
The story of how all things are, and here,

We needn't look very far.
Like this lonely flower here, reflections on my heart sear.
What had moved this all into place?
Controls all manner of time and space?
Continues to allow us to live by grace?
All creation brings Him glory, and we more so than this,
As humans here with a soul, created above all else in role,
Yet nothing still is disputable…
As the original creation is beautiful.

Short Stories

Tales of the Fruit Ninjas

Special thanks to Aaron Thomas. For it was your friendship that sparked the creation of this story, which, in turn, launched me into writing more.

Thank you.

Introduction

This crazy piece of fiction and nonsense is just a fun story based on two friends and their relationship. The outlandish events and the people involved are here for humor only and in no way reflect the nature or personality of the real-life people or characters depicted. All events read here are entirely fictitious and in no way represent the products or persons involved.

Before reading this story, you must understand the relationship between myself and Aaron. Aaron and I have been close friends since the winter of 2018. During our friendship, we share a mutual love of most Anime, fitness, and other miscellaneous things. However, we have had a friendly rivalry between us for most of our time knowing each other.

This book was initially supposed to just be a joke between Aaron and I. However, as it was being written, it got out of hand and has led to this final form. It is comprised of a combination of video game themes as well as anime references and parodies of various products and celebrities. And so, through the beckoning of my friends and family, something that was meant to never see the light of day, is here. In all its tasteless glory. Enjoy.

Chapter 1

It was cold and windy, not from my power but the external factors… but I must endure. I must push to be the best if I am ever to stand against A-Aron. Slash! A quick flash of red was seen. Another watermelon was lobbed at me and cut just as quickly. Whoosh! Slash! Apples and lemons next.

They kept coming, one after the other. I slashed through each one until I couldn't feel my arms, then I kept going beyond that. Each time they flew at me faster and faster, each one I cut down with a single stroke. The blessed blade, a powerful weapon that had been given to me for defeating the jelly 'giant' earlier on. Each of these trials gave me a new skill, each one a unique ability to master, but I would have to pull out my ace in the hole to beat this challenge, I think…

…Up until now, my rival A-Aron and I were about equally matched. Whether in workout movements, life skills, achievements, or otherwise, A-Aron and I went back and forth. I had come close once before, a long time ago now. I had used a tool I did not realize I could, and in the process, I humiliated him. However, to beat him thoroughly, I must get better. I scoured the ancient archives in search of the secret to the ultimate in humiliation weapons. Then, I found it. In the lowest pits of the tallest tower in the forgotten realm, there was my prize.

I faced many demons to claim it. The first one; the Racial Injustice Demon, he was an easy opponent and quickly ridden with my White Privilege ability. The next one, a slightly more menacing foe; the Inequality Monster. This one took some cunning, but I finally survived by wrapping myself with the cloak of non-binary orientation. Once through them, I faced the last one on the bottom floor guarding the access to my goal. This one, I thought, would take all my strength, and if I could beat her, I knew I was well on my way to finding my final form, the power-up ability to rid me of my rival forever.

The Black-Trans-Lesbian-Christian-Redneck. An interesting foe as they come, we fought gun for gun, jumping around the dungeon room using every gun or bullet ability I had, curving bullets, eagle eye shots, and quick draw. Nothing worked, her redneck country ability kept her on par with my skill. No standard weapon or ability would work here since she was just the contradiction of all of them in one. Then I tried to do some of my other special skills, but all fell short there as well. So I came up with something that came as a desperate last attempt… I befriended her.

Yes, I befriended the Black-Trans-Lesbian-Christian-Redneck, and throughout my time in the dungeon, I made her feel accepted and loved, and once I had her on the string, I knew how my plan would unfold. As she continued to believe that I was her friend, I brought her to the point mentally that she would do anything for me, and so she finally let me see the room where the texts were kept. Once inside, I found what I wanted, the crystals and texts that would show me the way to my final form. The one I needed was a pink crystal-like rock.

Upon leaving the room, I was greeted by the monster now friend still waiting in her dungeon area. Realizing then that her friendship was used only to give me what I wanted and nothing more. "Nooo!" she shrieked, echoing through the entire tower. A cold chill went up my spine, no, I thought, I did not come all this way to claim my prize now only to lose it.

But it seems fate was on my side. The Black-Trans-Lesbian-Christian-Redneck found out that the glass ceiling was real, even for her, and she would never be loved for who she was. Only what she could give and do for others. An icon appeared on my screen 'New ability unlocked' – 'Glass Ceiling Effect' – below was the paragraph describing the details of this ability and how everything I had done to this beast fit the description.

"Level up," a voice echoed in my mind and momentarily overrode the screams still coming from the beast in front of me. With a final shriek, after what seemed like several minutes of anguishing torment, she let out a yell and vanished, never to be seen again. A cold wind blew through the dungeon. Even my coat could not stop it from piercing my bones.

After escaping the tower, I found an old hunting cabin by a lake on the forgotten realm border. Here I meditated to open the crystal and get the information I so desired. After several hours of trying to get through, I finally got it to activate.

Almost telepathically, it told me the way. The final form, my ultimate humiliation weapon would be to dual wield the Fruity Feet whip strips. I had heard about this power before when I accidentally discovered the whip strips when I used it against A-Aron in one of our previous duels. It proved to be the most effective considering. I was extremely excited to see how I could attain the power to wield two at once. The first part of the journey was to face the jelly giant in the strawberry fields to the south. Thereupon his defeat, I would be granted a gift that would allow me to continue my journey headed south.

Chapter 2

The strawberry fields were pretty to look at but dangerous to walk through. Many creatures lurked beneath the leaves to the strawberries. The giant, however, should be easy to spot, I figured. I had been walking for about two days when I finally found what I was looking for, though not in the way I expected. The 'giant' was only about three feet tall and looked more like a disfigured fruit gusher/gummy bear crossover. I wasn't even sure I'd found my target until it spoke. "Who are you that enters my domain?" the creature said with a loud voice that sounded more female than male. The kind of voice that you would probably hear from someone who demanded to meet the manager.

"I am Lord Thomas," I started, bellowing a loud yet low rumble in my voice. "From the eastern lands I have traveled a…"

"Lord Thomas!" the creature interrupted. "You don't belong here, and if you don't go, I'll attack."

I held my ground, silent and still. The wind blew, the sweet aroma of strawberries in the air. I was staring down at it, and it was staring up at me. Punt! "Ahhhhhh," it cried faintly as it flew away. I stood there; my foot still raised in the air. I just punted a midget, I thought to myself, chuckling as I did so.

The creature was still falling some distance away, as I gazed out to watch when she hit the ground; a loud wet pop like a water-balloon burst sounded. Red jelly shot up almost as tall as me. "That was... legitimately disappointing," I said out loud to myself.

As I walked over to the impact point, I saw the jelly pile and the destroyed strawberry plants around it. In the center was a katana, stuck in the ground like Excalibur from the old stories. I pulled it out without much trouble, the blade glowed red in my hand. A message popped up in front of me: 'Proceed to the processing factory to the east.'

When I arrived, I was immediately greeted with various fruit flying at me; as a reflex, I dodged what I could and cut through the others...

...Now, here I stand my ground, eager to gain the next level in experience to gain control of the Fruity Feet Whip Strips. However, with this challenge, I would have to pull out my ace in the hole. Point! Point! Each time I cut the fruit apart, I heard the word. Slash! Whoosh! I continued to strike.

Without even realizing what was going on, I found myself cutting each fruit as it came, some melons, some apples, citrus, even the small grapes I had to cut them to be counted to win. I didn't know how long it was till I was done, no clock, no apparent overseer, and no opponent... just fruit. When at last I felt I could not feel or move my arms any more, they came harder, so I decided to use one of my abilities; I only got one shot with this one, I thought, as the air whirled around me. All the fruit was knocked away that even tried to come close.

I held the sword horizontally in front of me with my right hand, and with my left, I activated my power. A blue hue came from my palm as I called out, "Bordon Damsey!" Suddenly, the image of Bordon Damsey as a faint specter illuminated behind me.

"Fucker has pulled out his ace in the hole," Bordon said, echoing in the wind around me.

"Ultimate Chef, into the sword!" I yelled as I put my left hand on the sword blade, making the blade change from red to blue. My stamina regained, and "level up" was heard above me. New skills and abilities were unlocked, but I dismissed these messages until my current task was done.

Slash, swoosh! With a new lightning speed, I cut every fruit, multiple fruit at once, all with the precision accuracy of the master chef with a kitchen knife. We kept slashing dodging, my sword glowing blue, and my hair now pure white matching my eyes. I jumped, dodged, and cut through every fruit they could muster. Until suddenly, they stopped.

"Pass," was all I heard. No icons, no further messages. Bordon Damsey left my sword to take the form of the faint ghostly specter in front of me on his own accord. The sword returned to its red hue, and my hair and eyes, back to their original color of dark brown and green.

"You were a worthy host, Lord Thomas," Bordon said, "not like the idiot sandwiches I am used to."

"Thank you," I replied, and with that, he vanished. Leaving me to stare at the emptiness of the building in front of me. "Where did the fruit even come from?" I asked myself.

I started to venture in, and as I took a few steps towards the building, suddenly the message screen popped up – 'Level Complete.' – Venture to the top of the Dragon Mountain. As I looked to my right towards the southern end of the realm, I could see the mountain. Everyone knows about it. No one goes up it.

Chapter 3

As I walked towards the mountain, I went back through my messages from the level up that I received earlier. One of the skills unlocked was the Fruit Taffy shield. Unlike the Fruity Feet weapon that I used, this was squarer in shape and had designs in it. The full effect of this I had yet to discover.

When I reached the Dragon Mountain, it echoed with an eerie chill. I began to walk up the mountain path, if you could call it a path. As I climbed, I activated 'Fruit Boost', which enabled me to climb as though gravity wasn't a thing.

When I reached a summit, I found a temple-like structure. Inside, it was empty; ghostly echoes of the wind could be heard throughout it. In the center was a room, empty like the others, except for the etchings on the floor that looked like a giant juicy burst gummy. I sat down in the center and attempted to meditate after the long journey upwards.

Snap! Something hit me; I looked around. A jellybean was on the floor near my lap. "Strange," I said quietly to myself. I began to meditate again. Snap! Again, then before I could gather my thoughts, several at once. A barrage of jellybeans with stinging force came at me from nowhere. Unable to stand it, I fell to the floor, curled up, buying time to think, "Fruit Taffy shield," I activated.

The barrage stopped hitting me and stopped short at the shield that was now around me. A solid barrier of fruit taffy with unicorn designs encompassed my body. It was blocking all the jellybeans. Unsure of how long it would last, I began to meditate right away. As I got into my meditative state, I heard the faint voice singing, "If you come with me, you will see."

"Billy Bonka!" I gasped. His presence was now clearly in front of me. The Fruit Taffy shield had grown out away from me to increase the shield circumference. Inside it now, Bonka and I stood eye to eye.

"What is it that you seek?" he asked me.

"The ultimate in humiliation weapons," I replied. "To defeat my foe A-Aron and, at last, declare victory over his ideas that Naruto is a good anime. And that he could ever be as good as me."

Billy Bonka cringed at the thought. "I too," he started. "I too, wish that Naruto had never been made. The weapon you seek is in the center of the boiling gelatin lake at the center of this mountain. Going there is suicide."

"I must try. I need my final form if I am to beat him."

"I understand."

He pulled out a pipe and played a little tune. Suddenly, a very strange looking orange man rather plump in build appeared. "Take the lord to the entrance of the gelatin lake," Billy Bonka said. Then he looked to me. "A word of advice, your foe will be fought twice. And the final form is final because there is nothing above it. Once you have used it, there is no going back."

I nodded in understanding as the orange man and I vanished from sight. The fruit taffy shield disappeared with me, and the jellybean barrage stopped. Billy Bonka stood there alone, gazing at the spot where I stood. "Will he succeed?" he asked, glancing upward as if to be talking to someone above him.

"He will," came an ominous feminine reply.

A smile crept over Billy Bonka then, and with a twirl of his cane, he began singing again, trailing off as he walked away.

Meanwhile, I was suddenly sweltering as I materialized on the edge of the gelatin lake with the orange plump man. But as quickly as he appeared with me, he vanished, leaving me alone. Surveying my surroundings, I noticed a large landmass in the center of the lake, of course. I thought, just like the movies. I scroll through my inventory to see what I may have to help assist me here, nothing, maybe.

"Fruit Taffy shield," I said, and instantly, I was encompassed in the shield. I inched closer to the lake to test my theory. It held. The shield could be used as a hamster wheel, and I could run across the lake to the island in the center. But would it make the whole way? I wondered.

"Fruit boost," I said as I posed at the edge, ready to sprint with my shield still engaged. I ran. "Level up – two abilities used at once," the voice was faint but distinct. I ignored the message for now, I had to focus.

"Almost there," I muttered to myself. I was still sprinting with the fruit boost, using my shield to 'walk' on the lake. The boiling gelatin made it hotter than it should be. I was sweating buckets, still though; I pushed forward. I must become more, I thought to myself, my desire to finally end my foe boiling as hot as the gelatin I walked on. When I neared the edge of the island in the center, I realized that my fight was far from over. Waiting for me on the shore of this island, A-Aron!

"What's this?" I yelled out as I approached the shore. A-Aron, or a form of him at least. Same figure, but different in appearance. This one was black, like jet ink black with white highlights and some grey shadows in his movements. We stared at each other for what seemed like an eternity. Then the silence was broken.

"I am Nega-Ron!" he started to say. My expression changed to a puzzled look as he continued, "I am Negative A-Aron. The negative essence of A-Aron here to keep you from your prize, my lord." the figure ended that sentence with such heavy sarcasm anyone would see he just mocked me on my title. My lord, I thought, repeating his tone in my head. "I am the guardian of the final form," he continued. "Formed in fear of what you hate most."

That makes sense, I thought, he's just a shadow of what A-Aron is to me. Reflected here, he takes the negative side of that person. "You must be defeated," I said aloud, and with that, I drew my sword. Glowing red and ready in my hand. 'Steady-Hand: activated,' 'Blocking Boost: Enabled,' the messages flashed before me as I engaged them, prepared to fight.

Nega-Ron barely moved. He remained calm and still. The wind circling my feet moved my coat in the breeze, my energy level increased, and the dust on the ground lifted a little, spinning with the wind. Tense and ready, I posed, waiting for his move. "Dartin Ruther Wing!" Nega-Ron yelled as his energy level spiked!

'White Privilege has been disabled' – the message flashed across my screen. Thankfully, I had not been relying on that one. Though I did hope I could use it later if it came to it. The air continued to move faster around A-Aron. "He still has no weapon," I muttered. Then, suddenly Nega-Ron raised his right arm and, in his hand, materialized a sword as I have never seen, physically bigger than one man could hold. If this was a shadow of the original Nega-Ron, then how much power does he have? Or a better question, how much is he still holding back? I thought to myself. Neither warrior moved. Energy and wind circled, each one blowing their coats. What is he waiting for? I thought.

Then suddenly, he attacked. We collided swords again and again from every angle. I barely blocked them, but I managed to hold my ground. The size of his sword was crushing. With each hit, it sent massive vibrations all through my arms. Thankfully, my blocking skill was activated, or I don't think I would've been able to catch these hits. "Naruto is the best Anime," he said as we hit our swords together. Neither one was giving an inch to the other.

"Hellsing," I responded through my gritted teeth. We pushed away from each other and stood to reset our attack.

"You will not gain the upper hand here. Even if you defeat me here, you still must face me in the end, and then, you will fail," Nega-Ron stated.

"*...your foe will be fought twice...*" remembering what Billy Bonka told me before I left him. I will have to fight Nega-Ron then A-Aron to beat him.

"Your humiliation will come to an end here!" Nega-Ron continued.

"You always were second best!" I responded.

"Sobe!" Nega-Ron yelled and, as quick as he yelled, he pulled a gun from who knows where and shot.

"Hit," the voice said in my head. Armor integrity down Twenty percent.

"Shit," I said. "I didn't even see that coming."

Laughing could be heard from Nega-Ron. "Sobe never

misses."

I panicked for a moment but remembered I had received other items for defeating the fruit ninja level earlier. I quickly ran through my menu in my head and selected the juicy burst bombs. Nega-Ron stood about to attack, still smirking from his successful hit against me. Boom! Suddenly a small explosion went off by his feet. Sticky goo was all over his shoes and ankles, berry smelling goo. "Aww hell naw!" Nega-Ron cried out. "My new Jordans."

"Hit," the voice said in Nega-Ron's head. "Black Status Symbol: Destroyed, Armor Integrity: Compromised. Stamina: Decreased, Morale: Decreased."

I threw more juicy burst bombs, but Nega-Ron was quick on his feet now; we fought clashing swords and exchanging shots, neither of us getting far. "I must win," I repeated to myself to continue the fight. We each went shot for shot and sword to sword, almost perfectly matched. There was a strange unison and balance to our struggle as if we were trained by the same person and timed each move, not to kill, but to spar. Try as I might with varying attacks that Nega-Ron would counter with minimal effort, and I the same to him. This fighting went on for some time, still arguing as we fought.

"If you cannot see the error of your thinking about this show and your position to me, then you must die!"

"If that's your reasoning, then you are lost to me!" I replied as our swords clashed again. The gelatin boiling, shining a crystal white; the sheen around us was intense as we clashed, hot and blinding to us as we fought – neither making any ground.

Chapter 4

Time flew as we fought. I activated my Fruit Taffy shield, which made Nega-Ron take a hit of sorts, traumatized slightly from the incident so long ago, but it didn't faze him much. Nega-Ron struck my shield continuously. When its integrity was almost gone, I braced myself, but suddenly, the unicorn characters jumped off the taffy in a swift attack; they penetrated Nega-Ron as they ran through him.

'Last Defense: Enabled.' Nice, I thought as I dismissed the message. 'Level up, skill upgraded – White Privilege. Upgrade: Original form.' Original Form? I thought, what? Noticing that my White Privilege ability was unlocked, Nega-Ron quickly composed himself as best he could to counter.

"White Privilege!" I yelled, raising my sword in the air. Thunder rolled, and the earth shook.

Nega-Ron suddenly fell against his will and dropped to his knees, looked up at me and said, "What is thy bidding my master?"

Neither of us could believe what just happened. Nega-Ron was held against his will yet, with his will. "Original form of white privilege?" I asked out loud. Then it hit me, 'slave'. Quickly I turned to look up towards the top of the hill at the cave that I must get to to find my weapon. Turning to Nega-Ron, still struggling to stand up and fight off this spell on him, I asked, "Is the weapon there?" Pointing to the cave on the hill. He would be forced to reveal it to me in this state.

"Yes," he replied begrudgingly.

I ran. "Fruit Boost," I cried as I ran up the embankment toward my goal. Nega-Ron still at the bottom muttering to himself. Trying every spell, he had to break free until he found it.

"Dichael Lackson: Activated." Going from black to white, the Dichael Lackson ability gave him the power to be completely free from any white privilege hits. "Nuhammad Oli," A-Aron yelled out as he chased after me. I was running fine; I didn't even notice that Nega-Ron was free now and on my trail. Until suddenly.

OOOFFF... Crash! I found myself peeling off the edge of the cave wall at the entrance, and Nega-Ron stood there, the light from the lake shone behind him, making his blackness look almost intimidating now. His eyes were fire. He held his fist up, still poised from when he hit me into the wall. I dropped to my knees and collected my wits. "Damn," I said. "If this is Nega-Ron, how is A-Aron going to be? I must get my final form."

We fought again, hand to hand. Exchanging blows until both of our lives were almost spent. I started to gain the upper hand when I found my moment. "Reality Check – Raw Deadlift," I said as I held Nega-Ron in my hands pinned against the wall of the cave. 'Hit, Deadlift score initiated.' Nega-Ron fought back, but his power was gone; he knew that already. He could not stand to my deadlift number, not even close, and so, with so much of his health already gone, he faded out into nothing.

"You haven't won yet, my lord," Nega-Ron said as he faded away, using the same sarcastic tone that was used before. I stood still, exhausted and hot. I collected myself enough and ventured into the cave. The aroma of fruit was heavy in the air, too many kinds to distinguish which ones were there.

As I entered the central room, it glowed brightly from the source in the center. Another crystal, this one though, looked like a giant red spoon. About as big as my arm. There a voice congratulated me on my victory thus far. "Who's there? And what just happened?" I asked out loud.

"I may have the answers to the questions you seek," said the voice from behind me. I whirled around, to come face to face with.

"Retty Rocker?" I exclaimed, half questioning my eyes.

"Yes," she replied. "It is I. I who have created all this, and I who have set you on your path." She continued, "You have been searching for the dual wield ability of the Fruity Feet strips. And here you will find it. I knew when I saw you so brilliantly use one against A-Aron that you would be the one who could reach this point and attain the power of two."

I kneeled humbly. "I have served, and I will continue to serve."

"Lord Thomas, you are hereby granted the power of the Fruity Feet dual wield ability," Retty Rocker started to say. "Furthermore, you are granted the additional abilities and the spirit guides to assist you in defeating your foe." Retty paused before continuing. "Your sword?" she asked. I handed her my sword, and she held it and knighted me with it. When she tapped my shoulder, I saw the pop-ups. 'Level up, level up.' the messages continued to pop up and flash before me.

When she handed me back my sword, its curved blade was straight, the black handle, now white, and the glowing red blade, a shining black. My clothes changed my hair, all my stats. I stood holding a Fruity Feet in each hand. Wild berry energy coursing through my arms. It was electrifying! The sensation I felt. Now, I thought, now I can beat him.

"It's time," she said. And with that, she vanished, and I was suddenly teleported out and back to the realm of my home, to the realm of A-Aron and our final battle.

"This is the end for you, A-Aron," I said to myself.

I could only hope.

Chapter 5

Back in the city, A-Aron could feel the power shift and was already planning for the attack. "A-Aron!" I yelled. Using an energy boost to enhance my voice across the city.

"On your left!" a voice cried out from behind me. I turned quickly to look. A-Aron was already in full swing, coming up behind me with a sword three times his size. A quick draw of my sword and I deflected the blow. Clash! Our swords met, and even though I blocked it, the impact still sent me flying to the side. We repeatedly clashed until our fighting had taken us far outside the city to the open fields…

A-Aron suddenly attacked from above. I deflected and quickly reset and faced my opponent. We paused, each of us, gauging the other. The sun shone on my now white attire adorned with black trim, long hair flowing in the wind. A-Aron stood opposite me and had his classic black on black, his hair shining in the sun from how it reflected the tight waves in his hair.

"Auntie Gema!" A-Aron suddenly yelled. There was a flash of light, and she appeared behind him in the specter form just as Bordon Damsey had for me earlier on. The spirit moved around him, and I could feel his energy rising. I tried to attack, but I couldn't even get near him. "Auntie Gema. Syrup attack!" A-Aron shouted as the energy calmed, just long enough for her attack to come at me.

"Fruit taffy shield," I yelled. Crash! Just as the syrup

attack hit me, I was covered by the shield. The tension was strong and steady. "Last Defense!" I cried out, and the unicorns in the fruit taffy launched out. A-Aron managed to deflect some, but it gave me time to escape the attack that currently still pounded my shield.

Once clear, I launched the juicy burst bombs, A-Aron suddenly felt a cold chill of a defeat possibility, but he managed to hold his own. Splat! Right on his head, the juicy burst landed and blew up, destroying his perfect wave hair. 'Hit. Signature Look: Destroyed. Morale: Decreased, Brother-Status: Decreased.' A lucky shot if there was one. I figured I didn't have too many of those. I used that hit as my moment to strike. I lunged forward, sword at the ready. But A-Aron was too good and used an ability that I don't have, high jump.

Natural to his nature, A-Aron has the ability to high jump by mere thought, and it never runs out. "Shit," I said, glancing up at A-Aron in the air.

Suddenly another syrup attack was headed straight for me! Auntie Gema was still hovering nearby, and her onslaught was pressing. "Silly Ways!" I shouted quickly, and his specter appeared.

"Hi, Silly Ways here…" he started to say.

I quickly cut him off. "Into the sword!" I shouted. Immediately, my sword took the form of a brush. "Special attack number five: Oxygen-Cleaning!" I cried. As fast as I said it, and just in time, Oxygen-Cleaning was released in thunderous waves and decimated the syrup attack and Auntie Gema all at once. A-Aron, now back on the ground, furious at his defeat here, pressed his attack.

I was already ready for him, still with the spirit of Silly Ways in my sword now brush. "Special attack number three:

Orange Power!" I shouted. The ground became slicker than shit as A-Aron ran forward right into the attack. He slipped but not as much as he should have.

"But wait, there's more!" Silly's spirit cried out as he launched another round of attacks. The cleaning product Explosion pummeled A-Aron with all intensity.

No one could survive this, I thought to myself. I may not even need the dual wield ability. The aftermath of the attack left a small crater in the ground. As I walked closer to the crater, I looked and saw him, struggling but alive.

"Naruto doesn't deserve the attention it gets," I said to him. "And you will always be second best. Surrender now, don't make me bring out my final form."

"But my lord," A-Aron started to say, his head still bowed to the ground as he kneeled there using the same sarcastic tone as the Nega-Ron I faced earlier. "If I surrender, who will ever put you in your place?" As A-Aron finished, he stood up and faced me from the bottom of the crater.

"Don't try it," I said.

"You underestimate my power," A-Aron replied. Then he jumped. With his high jump activated again, he cleared the crater and continued to climb over me. I jumped to meet him in the air, but as I did, I heard him say, "Muscle-up strength!" Suddenly my strength suffered a blow, and I fell to the ground.

'Hit.' A-Aron used 'Reality Check: Muscle-Up Strength.'

'Stamina: Decreased, Morale: Decreased, Will to Live: Decreased.' "Blast it," I said to myself as the messages rolled past my face. "He knows I can't get that movement down, and the fact that he has continued to keep him that one step above me." A-Aron landed some yards away, his clothes torn and tattered from the barrage he just survived. The wind circled him as he stood, his energy still surging around him. I managed to pick myself up, still weak from that last attack.

"I'm disappointed," A-Aron started, "that we couldn't be just as we are, but Naruto is a great anime." He finished. "I will ascend."

It was now or never… my final form.

Chapter 6

Energy crackled around me. The fruit aroma was suddenly strong and distinct. The air moved around, picking the dust off the ground. A-Aron stood there, nervous, but ready. He knew what was coming. As the ability unfolded, the fruity feet extended in each hand. Three feet of surging wild berry fruit energy. The white clothes I had turned to tie-dye, colorful electric shocks randomly traveled the surface of the clothes. "Toasted Pastry attack!" A-Aron shouted nervously.

"Fruit Taffy shield!" I stated in reply. The pastries hit hard, hot, and fast, as if straight out of the toaster. But my shield held for now. I ran towards the attack and to A-Aron, whips in hand fruit flavor energy to the maximum. We fought, clashing, and dodging each other whips to pastries. Neither one of us genuinely gaining ground. Crack! Crack! The whips sounded like thunder breaking up the environment wherever they made contact. Boom! Crash! The toasted pastries exploded everything they hit.

After what seemed like an eternity fighting, I finally grabbed his face with a whip and pulled him down towards me, sending fruity shocks continuously at him. 'Hit, Humiliation Attack: Activated, Morale: Decreased, Stamina: Decreased, Energy Level: Draining.' The messages popped up on A-Aron's screen as he wrestled against it, almost pulling away until I got one of his arms with my other whip. He was down, for the moment.

"Do not resist," I told him. "Don't make this worse."

"You won't do it," A-Aron replied.

"Watermelon flavor," I stated defiantly.

Instantly A-Aron went numb, crazed as if being electrocuted, tormented by the flavor he can't, by nature, resist. The torment continued for a few moments as I saw his stats decreasing steadily. "Almost," I muttered.

In his last breath, A-Aron managed to mutter a single phrase... "Naruto is great, Hellsing is okay, but Bleach is better than both."

My eyes went wide as I froze. Did he really just say this? Can we settle on our mutual love of Bleach and not focus on the dislikes between us? I stopped my attack. The wind and energy that had been blowing around us stopped. The dust settled. I looked at him lying there, mostly dead; and he, looking up at me. "Let us unite in our common love of the Bleach anime. Instead of us fighting for the better show," A-Aron muttered softly.

I looked at the whips in my hands and realized that indeed we were the same, with only small differences. "Yes," I replied. "We can."

"Level Up." Both of us heard the message.

'Interracial Bro Factor: Enabled, Teamwork: enabled. Stamina: Increased. Energy Levels; Restored. Energy Levels: Increased, New Abilities: Unlocked.' The messages were extensive. The abilities we unlocked with this move were insane. And now both of us would be impervious to all kinds of attacks since we now fought together.

"Nooooo!" the thunderous cry of an older woman echoed throughout the air. Both A-Aron and I glanced around quickly. Until we saw her. Or rather, them.

As A-Aron and I turned around, we saw Retty Rocker, but she wasn't alone this time. With her was Waula Bean, Lachel Fay, and Bartha Lewart. The energy readings were off the charts, collectively over nine thousand. A-Aron and I looked at each other and then back at the ladies. "What does this mean?" I asked. "To what end is this scheme of yours?" No reply was given at first.

"We are here to finish the job that you couldn't," Retty Rocker finally said. "To rid the world of A-Aron and force the rivalry to continue between you, both white and black."

Chapter 7

A-Aron and I stood together now, two against the four. A-Aron was now wearing bright new Jordans, with slightly baggy black pants and a skin-tight white shirt. His hair went full brother mode as his tight waves changed to a full afro with a white headband tied around his head, its long tails blowing in the wind. His sword had reappeared in his hand still three times his size. He stood next to me, ready but casual. My attire had also changed in the level up process, black boots with white pants, black belt, and tight white shirt with black accents. My hair still long but tied up in a ponytail with some loose strands by my face. My sword was back in my hand as well, same as before but slightly bigger now with our new power level.

    The ladies stood ready, then, one by one, they called out, and with each cry the energy around them was building and building. "Nobody can cook as good as your mama!" yelled Waula Bean. As the air swirled around her, the rolling pin in her hand grew to the size of an oversized baseball bat.

    "Yum-O!" yelled Lachel Fay next; the air was also swirling around her. A meat tenderizer grew in her hand, bigger than her head, yet she swung it with ease as she stood there, letting her energy level build.

    "Life is too complicated not to be orderly!" yelled Bartha Lewart next. "I'm ready to toss your salad!" she continued to say in a menacing tone towards us. As she spoke, two giant salad forks appeared in her hands, each one almost as big as she is.

"Isn't tossing the salad my line?" I asked A-Aron quietly as the forks appeared in Bartha's hands.

A-Aron couldn't help but crack a chuckle under his breath. "There's definitely a joke in there," he replied.

"I knew I should've done this myself from the beginning," said Retty Rocker, closer to a regular speaking tone. A giant red wooden spoon was in her hand then as she continued, "You were supposed to be the tragedy that pushed society over the edge!"

A-Aron and I glanced at each other and then back up at her. "The boss said it would work! Yet here we are," Retty said. "If you had beaten him like you were supposed to," she said now, directing her gaze at me.

"What's so important about A-Aron's defeat to you?" I answered.

"His power is just so that it could just be what causes my downfall in cooking," Retty replied. "It just so happened that this fight worked to the boss's advantage, and they were going to use it to help further our causes together."

"Who's they?" A-Aron questioned.

"Not for you to worry about now," Bartha sneered.

"Butter Cannons!" Waula cried out suddenly. Without warning, a barrage of butter sticks was headed straight for A-Aron and me.

"Fruit Taffy shield!" A-Aron jumped in closer as I activated the shield. Over and over, each one, the butter hit a crushing hit against the shield and pushed us into the ground!

After a few minutes, Waula paused the attack for a moment. "Like I always say, 'never substitute butter'," she stated as the four glanced down at the hole where A-Aron and I just stood. Suddenly a massive surge of tie-dye color shot out of the crater at the ladies watching. The fruit scented colorful blast sent the women stumbling backward a bit as A-Aron, and I just stood there, seemingly untouched by Waula's butter cannons.

"Impossible!" Waula cried out.

"EVOO!" yelled Lachel Fay. Instantly a wave of extra virgin olive oil swept over the ground. 'High Jump: Activated' – A-Aron jumped and pulled me up with him, but Lachel Fay was already pressing her attack at us. Her giant meat tenderizer met our swords as we collided midair.

Bang! Crash! The metal's sound on metal was deafening as we fought, tumbling as we went towards the ground. "Fruit Boost!" I yelled as A-Aron, and I landed some distance safely away from the crater where we started. Lachel Fay landed near us, and, while not as graceful: unfortunately, unharmed. After we landed, Lachel was quick to press on again and surprisingly held her own against both A-Aron and I for a while as we continued to fight, swords against meat tenderizer.

"You aren't even tall," Waula Bean sneered at A-Aron as she got to the place where we were fighting. "You're a disgrace to your race, not even a proper black, just a ni…"

"White Privilege!" I yelled, interrupting her. 'Interracial Bro Factor: Enabled – White Privilege: Racial Equality: Active.' The message came loud and clear. Waula froze as she heard it.

'Hit. Morale: Decreased. Hidden weapon used – Reality Check: Social Media Backlash, Energy Level: Decreased, Come-back: Disabled, Status: Lost.' Now was our chance. Waula Bean was frozen as the response to her trying to use the 'n' word even against an enemy was met with a huge wave of unforeseen backlash. The other ladies stood shocked and pissed as they realized what was about to happen.

I launched the juicy burst bombs. Waula took the hits. Every. Single. One. As each juicy burst bomb splattered on her, she started to look like the recipient of a colorful bukkake session; colorful fruit scented goo all over her face and body. "A-Aron, now!" I said to him.

"Sobe!" yelled A-Aron as he pulled out his gun and shot. While my bombs did their thing, further draining her health and energy levels, it was A-Aron's shot that took it home. Dead center shot. And Waula Bean fell; no sound or word was heard from her. For as she hit the ground, she vanished just as quickly.

"Flawless Victory! Level Up!" the voices echoed in both A-Aron's and my mind.

Lachel Fay, who was closest to the event, stood wide-eyed. The other ladies were frozen as well. A-Aron and I took that moment to pause and wait for them to make their move. Do we keep fighting? I thought. It didn't take long to find out. Lachel Fay burst out and lunged at me, separating A-Aron and me. Before A-Aron could help, Bartha Lewart was already charging him.

Crash! A-Aron met her head-on, sword to salad fork, as Lachel Fay and I went head-to-head. Retty Rocker just stood off in the distance, watching. The loss of Waula Bean so quickly meant that she needed to be more careful. Having us split up, to Retty, seemed the better option now.

As Lachel Fay pressed her attack, our weapons clashing, and neither one was gaining any ground. We finally clashed and sent each other flying away. Catching ourselves, we turned to face each other. "Choup and Stoup!" Lachel yelled as she swung her hammer hard at the ground. As the hammer hit the ground, it started to crack from her to me, and out of the cracks, it began to ooze then spout a weird chowder soup blend.

As I cautiously tried to avoid the cracks and the ooze, I ran through my inventory. Shit, I thought. Then I realized, 'Shit' – That was the ability. To turn any weapon into a shit weapon. I composed myself quickly and switched my sword from the right to my left hand and slammed my right hand to the ground and yelled, "Shit!" As I yelled, I stood up and threw my arm towards Lachel. Instantly the ooze turned to poop and shot back at her. Lachel seemed unfazed as she jumped to dodge and spun around, swinging her tenderizer as she went.

As she came around to face me again, she yelled, "Pet Food!" As a counter-spell, swinging her tenderizer in the air like a baseball bat pretending to hit the shit turned pet food towards me.

Just as fast as the shit was headed for her, it was turned back at me in the form of dog and cat food. I was ready now and stood facing her with my sword still in my left hand, and my right held straight out towards her. Just before the shit would make an impact, I countered back and called out, "Reality Check!" Unsure of the effects it would choose, I figured Lachel had something that would take a hit and cause her attack to cease. Unless you know a specific weakness, calling out 'reality check' on its own would automatically find one – if it was present – and then use it against the target. With Lachel Fay, I could only hope it would work.

Seconds seemed like minutes as the effect of the spell

took shape. 'Hit, – Lord Thomas used Reality Check – Not a Professional Chef, Lifestyle Status: Corrupted, Energy Level: Decreased.' The messages scrolled past Lachel's face, and as it did so, the pet food dropped harmlessly to the ground. Her face showed instant pain as she fell forward – leaning on her meat tenderizer weapon, which was now shrinking back to standard size; albeit slowly.

'Secret Exposed – Humiliation attack points added, Hit. Morale: Decreased, Will to live: Decreased, Energy Level: Decreased.' The messages continued to roll past her face as she fell to the ground. At that time, I walked over to her. The ground still cracked from her attack before, and pet food was strewn about as I stood over her. She knelt on the ground, still clinging to her weapon like a crutch or cane, as it continued to shrink.

"You were always just a shadow in the world of master chefs," I said to her. With a smooth stroke of my sword, I cut off her head. Before it hit the ground, she was already fading away.

Chapter 8

Meanwhile. A-Aron and Bartha Lewart were still going at it head-to-head.

Clash! Clang! The sword sounds were quick and robust between Bartha and A-Aron. He could see Lachel Fay and I were going at it and then continued to focus on Bartha Lewart. She didn't give him any leeway as they fought, but no matter how much Bartha tried, she couldn't get an opening to make a good hit against A-Aron.

As they continued to fight, A-Aron managed to break away for a moment and collect himself, and Bartha did the same. Then suddenly, without warning, she cried out, "Fruit Salad!" Instantly dozens of various fruits came flying at A-Aron with incredible speed. A-Aron dodged and sliced each one as best he could. He wouldn't last long unless he thought of something quick.

"Bedna Lewis!" A-Aron cried out. The elderly famous black chef appeared as Auntie Gemima did for him earlier. The air swirled around him as Bedna's spirit form appeared and grew to full size. The fruit that was pummeling A-Aron fell short of their target as Bedna kept them at bay with her power. "Bedna Lewis," A-Aron said quickly. "Favorite recipe." Immediately the spirit of Bedna held an open book in her hands, and the pages flipped with lightning speed. With a flash of light, the power came from the pages and immediately encompassed A-Aron and Martha's area.

"Fruit salad, you say?" came Bedna's voice through the bright glow that was entirely around them. "You haven't seen anything yet." Suddenly, the momentarily frozen fruit was now sucked into a central spot in front of A-Aron. The light and energy dimmed a bit, and you could see Bartha and A-Aron now some distance apart with Bedna in between them. In front of her was a small glowing mass where the fruit had been collected. Bartha tried to fight back and pushed more fruit at the spirit. It didn't matter. Everything was immediately sucked into the glowing mass of light Bedna had in front of her. "Try my recipe on for size," yelled Bedna, as she blasted with such tremendous force back at Bartha Lewart. The energy of fruit was intense as it pummeled her as she stood there.

Bartha held her own, though. "Is that it? Is this all you can conjure A-Aron?" Bedna didn't slow down her attack, and A-Aron just stood still but tense in response to Bartha's questions. "I know how to roll a joint." Bartha sneered, still bracing herself against the blast.

Bedna's attack stopped. A-Aron knew that he would have to try something different. "A joint you say? Noop Doggy!" he called out. Without missing a beat, Noop Doggy appeared. And with him, a cloud of smoke around his figure. A soft hip hop beat started to play.

You call my name,
Now I'm here to play.
You might think it's a game,
But I'm here to slay.

Noop Doggy would rhyme as he spoke with a flow so smooth that no one could resist. His trance was magic. A-Aron knew he could beat her now. Bartha was immediately taken aback. As Noop Doggy walked closer, Bartha softened her defense, entranced by his rhyme and, combined with the smoke she inhaled as he got closer. She was losing, and she didn't even know it.

'Hit. Hip Hop Flow: Activated, Energy: Decreased, Stamina: Decreased. Hidden ability activated – Mary Jane, Defense: Disabled, Speed: Decreased, Inhibitions: Disabled.'

A-Aron knew this was his chance. As Noop Doggy did his thing, Bartha Lewart had dropped her guard and all sense of attack. "Reality Check!" A-Aron shouted, holding his left hand out towards Bartha and his sword held casually in his right.

'Hit. A-Aron used Reality Check – Insider Trading.' Bartha suddenly felt the impact and burst up, but it was too late. 'Lifestyle Status: Corrupted, Energy Level: Decreased.' The messages flashed across Bartha's face. 'Secret Exposed – Humiliation attack points added, Hit. Morale: Decreased, Will to live: Decreased, Energy Level: Decreased.' She was finished. Noop vanished in the puff of smoke as A-Aron walked up to Bartha, who was now curled on the ground in pain.

"Just a wanna-be has been," A-Aron said as she looked up to him from the ground. Slash! A quick flick of the wrist and A-Aron's sword cut Bartha clean in two, having her vanish just as I reached him from finishing Lachel Fay.

"One more," I said, just catching my breath as I reached A-Aron.

"Let's get it," A-Aron replied. Retty Rocker stood off in the distance, watching. She wasn't too concerned that A-Aron and I beat the others. However, she was worried about what the boss would say…

Chapter 9

Big Media has had the plan to continue to have a racial divide across the lands. Realizing the conflict that A-Aron and I had given off, Retty Rocker approached them and told them of our feud, and with that, the Big Media plan could be set. They took Retty's idea and decided to play that card and see how much they could spin-off to keep the rest of the people tied in the race wars.

Retty Rocker told them of how she discovered what she called a 'Fruit Ninja'. She said that this discovery laid the foundations for her to set up the means to ensure that A-Aron would fall, and the Big Media's plan for a race war would continue. And so, she set to work, pouring all of her malice and desire into the 'Final Form', the weapon the Fruit Ninja could use to bring the ultimate humiliation against A-Aron. Secretly she had sent out the Philadelphia Cookie-Dough Boy to leave subtle hints that Lord Thomas would take, and it had worked thus far. The tips and whispers led Lord Thomas to the forgotten realm, where he started his trek to find the 'Final Form'.

Secretly though, Retty Rocker was afraid of what would happen should A-Aron get a hold of her powers. And the culinary master that would come from it. She was more determined to eliminate A-Aron than pursue the feud of Big Media's race wars. However, she needed their help to make it happen…

...But now, as these thoughts raced through her mind, Retty faced the cruel reality of what happened in front of her. She was worried; she didn't show it, no, she was far too old and stubborn for that. But she had not counted on the friendship of A-Aron with Lord Thomas to overcome the rivalry, team up, and take out her team together. This was no good.

While the fight was going on in front of her with A-Aron going head-to-head with Bartha Lewart and Lord Thomas with Lachel Fay and Waula Bean already gone. Retty quickly called for aid. You didn't see it, you couldn't hear it, but the call went out none the less. In the hollow echoes of the Forgotten Realm in the temple on the Dragon Mountain, it was heard. "Bring your army and your skills," Retty's voice echoed in the empty temple.

"We make the music, and we dream the dreams," Billy Bonka's voice echoed back. Nobody was seen, no figure in the temple, just hollow voices.

...The fight continued in front of Retty Rocker as she watched with intent. We must win, she thought to herself. When A-Aron and I finished off our opponents. She poised herself and began to walk towards us slowly. The remnants of the fighting were still strewn about. Craters and cracks in the ground with pet food and fruit pieces lying around. A-Aron and I headed towards Retty, ready and cautious of what could happen. As we got closer, we noticed Retty's typical red outfit was much darker now. The red spoon in her hand was oversized, but not like the weapons of the other ladies.

"Are you ready to call it quits?" A-Aron asked as we approached.

"I don't quit anything," Retty Rocker responded. "You

haven't seen all that I will do, and you won't survive what's coming."

Without warning, a massive wave of various fruits was launched at us out of nowhere – watermelons, apples, pineapples, and more. A-Aron and I slashed continuously, dodging some while cutting others. For a moment, it seemed hopeless, as we cut down everyone we could.

"Fruit Taffy shield!" I yelled, and instantly both A-Aron and I were encompassed by the protective layer. But it wouldn't last long, as the barrage of fruit came, it became clear that this shield wouldn't hold forever against Retty Rocker's fruit. I would have to time it just right. 'Last Defense: Enabled,' the message flashed before me. I nodded to A-Aron, who stood ready next to me, as the unicorns shot out and made the area clear for a moment and left Retty to defend against them.

"Fruit Boost!" I called out and grabbed A-Aron, as I did, pulling us away from the fight to regroup. As we glanced back to see what happened, we noticed that while the last defense unicorns destroyed the fruit blast momentarily, they did nothing to Retty.

"How can this be?" A-Aron asked himself as I just stood speechless and curious about what happened.

"Did you think my own creation would actually hurt me?" Retty sneered at us as she walked closer. "I created the Fruit Taffy. I can control the effects of the weapon."

Suddenly she stopped, and with a wave of her giant red spoon, she summoned a dark batter-like substance. The energy and batter swirled around her as A-Aron, and I watched, tense and ready. With a flick of the wrist, she launched the batter at us. A-Aron and I managed to dodge the initial hit, but it tumbled at us continuously until we started taking hits.

'Hit. Brownie Batter: Activated, Stamina: Decreased, Reaction Time: Decreased, Energy Level: Decreased.' The messages flew past our faces as we fought. "We must have something that we can use," A-Aron shouted to me as we both struggled to move amongst the brownie batter around us.

"Perhaps," I replied. "Mr. Scrubbing," I shouted as the batter started to encompass us fully.

Boom! The vibrations shook the ground. Retty Rocker braced herself but didn't seem too distraught about it. Immediately after the explosion, Mr. Scrubbing appeared in specter form, his whiteness shone like the sun. His mere presence forced the power of the brownie batter to start to recede. A-Aron and I were both finally able to break free of it standing behind him. "You don't frighten me, bald man!" said Retty as she poised for an attack against him.

"Perhaps not," Mr. Scrubbing replied. White erasers suddenly appeared in his hands, as they did, so his hands glowed, and the energy came out, and the brownie batter started to be cleaned, as if it never happened.

Retty Rocker wasn't moved. "Red Velvet," she said and waved her spoon at Mr. Scrubbing. The Red Velvet attack took Mr. Scrubbing by surprise, his white clothes suddenly stained red. The more stains he took, the more his power weakened.

"Danielle Amoss!" A-Aron yelled suddenly. I turned quickly to look in his direction, puzzled at his idea. A-Aron just nodded back, half-smiling as he did.

Before I could think of a response to that, the smell of

pine cleaning solution was in the air, so strong it took over the fruit smell that had been lingering since the fight began. Then it hit, wave after wave of the pine cleaner washed over the area. Retty Rocker took some minor damage and stumbled back as she did. The red velvet and brownie batter were all gone. Mr. Scrubbing was regaining his strength as this happened.

"That's the power of pine scented cleaner, baby!" Danielle's voice said from the waves, and with that, it was gone. The pine smell, Mr. Scrubbing, the batter attack, all of it was gone. Retty Rocker stood off, pissed now that she lost this fight after being so close to winning. A-Aron and I stood facing her some distance away.

"I should probably try my fin…" I started to say to A-Aron, but I was interrupted by the unusual tremor in the ground, steady steps. It felt like each tremor paced right after the other. In the distance behind Retty Rocker, we saw them. Hundreds of them, little orange dwarf people, were marching together. Retty Rocker didn't even look back to see. She already knew what was there and smiled menacingly about it.

"What are they?" asked A-Aron.

I just shook my head. "Billy Bonka's army."

The army stood right behind Retty now, little orange men with green hair, no weapons, just them. Then we saw him, Billy Bonka himself showed up. Walking casually through the ranks until he stood side by side with Retty Rocker.

Chapter 10

The air was still. Retty Rocker and Billy Bonka stood against A-Aron and I in the field. The ground was torn apart, pieces of the last battles were everywhere. The only clean spot was not far to our right since that's where Mr. Scrubbing and Danielle Amoss had been. The fruit aroma was returning to the air, the smell of candy and sweet sugar as well.

"AHHHHHHH!" A-Aron shouted as he went to the max level. Tensing himself, he increased his power level, and with it, the air was spinning around him. The dust on the ground swirled with it. His afro changed back to his tight wave, his clothes stayed the same, but his sword grew again, now four times his size.

As the energy continued to build around A-Aron, I decided to try what I should have done earlier. "Final Form!" I yelled, and the energy around me spiked as well, just as before, my white clothes turned to tie-dye colors, Fruity Feet strips appeared in each hand, wild berry fruit energy crackling as they did, the electric shocks flowing across my body at random. As the energy levels stabilized, Billy Bonka and Retty Rocker stood silent but unalarmed.

With a quick tweet of his flute, Billy Bonka had set the little orange men on the path to war. They charged, obnoxiously and half stumbling as they came. A-Aron and I were ready. With loud cries, we charged back, two against hundreds. We were bound to lose, we were sure we would, but we knew we couldn't. We fought hard, whips cracking, sword slashing. Each one down was one less to go. As we hit them, they each would explode, and confetti would burst out like a piñata.

"Hooray!" was heard in the voices of children as each one of the orange men burst.

Using my increased energy level, I launched fruit gusher bombs in massive amounts. Each one exploded and took another man with it. A-Aron would pull his energy into his sword and as he slashed down a single stroke took out dozens a time.

"Hooray! Hooray! Hooray!" The chorus of children echoed. Confetti was everywhere. We were surviving, for now.

The fight continued in this way for some time as A-Aron and I fought. At this point, I had wrapped a whip around one of the faces of the orange men and was using him like a mace on the end of a chain, sending fruity electric shocks into it and swinging it about destroying others with it. Till after a few minutes of that, he finally burst as well.

"This is it," I said to A-Aron as we met and poised back-to-back. We pushed through and made it. Exhausted and worn, we stood together, A-Aron and I, and faced our final foes: Billy Bonka and Retty Rocker. They stood where they had started, some distance off, calm and collected. The aroma of Fruit was so strong it was almost gagging. The ground was littered with pieces of the burst orange men and confetti, so thick you could hardly see the ground in places. The energy levels had calmed but were still high around A-Aron and me.

Suddenly, I felt weak. The Fruity Feet whip strips in my hands disappeared. The tie-dye color in my clothes vanished as the white returned. I fell to the ground. A-Aron rushed to grab me as I fell. I dropped to my knees and then into his arms in his lap. Alive, but not moving, no sense of feeling… Darkness took me.

"What have you done?" A-Aron cried out at both Billy Bonka and Retty Rocker, who seemed pleased about the turn of events.

"I told him, there's no going back once you get the final form," Billy Bonka finally said.

"You think I gave him that power, and I can't just take it away?" Retty asked rhetorically. A-Aron glanced down at me then back up at them.

"It was all a game, A-Aron," said Billy Bonka taking a few steps closer. "We used you to help Big Media incite fear and continue the race war that it wants."

"Lord Thomas, the Fruit Ninja." Retty Rocker sighed. "Shame, he'd have made a great ally as such. I don't even think he knew of his potential. Oh well," she continued. "Guess we'll never know. Taking the power of the final form away is critically crippling."

"There's no way he'll survive," Billy Bonka interjected, finishing her thought.

"Finish him," said Retty menacingly towards Billy Bonka.

Billy Bonka continued to walk over, whistling as he did, he held his cane in his left hand. With his right, he grabbed the end and pulled it apart. A fine blade showed in the sun. A-Aron had started to put the pieces together, and his sadness turned to anger. His energy level rose again. Billy Bonka didn't seem too concerned, though, and was about to make the final blow with sword blade in his hand. With a slash of his sword, Billy Bonka made the movement clean. He cut down on Lord Thomas still in A-Aron's lap.

"No!" A-Aron yelled, and he ducked his head over Lord Thomas, stopping the blade. Billy Bonka didn't flinch as he thought he'd get two for one. Boom! the explosion sent Billy Bonka flying backward. A swirl of energy, colors, and fruit scents filled the air around A-Aron.

'Level up! Interracial Bro factor: Engaged! Sacrificial Love: Activated. Ultimate Defense: Activated. Level up! Secret Ability Unlocked: Public Praise! Energy Level: Increased.'

"Level up. Level up." The voices spoke so fast that you could hardly understand. A-Aron stood up, fruit flavor and tie-dye color swirled around him. Billy Bonka got up from where he fell back to and stared angrily at A-Aron. My limp body still next to him on the ground. Billy Bonka drove in to attack again, but A-Aron was already ready. He held up his hands and just softly said, "No."

Billy Bonka froze, 'Hit. Energy Level: Decreasing, Stamina: Decreasing.'

"What's going on?" yelled Retty at Billy Bonka.

"Candy may be dandy, but liquor works quicker," Billy Bonka replied solemnly. Realizing that he would lose, he sheathed his blade back in the cane and lifted his top hat off his head. A-Aron's sacrificial move had instantly swept over the area and started to drain the power level of Billy Bonka. The 'Public Praise' ability was the final blow that brought Billy Bonka to his end. Having the public praise for his sacrifice gave A-Aron the advantage he needed.

"Fruit Attack!" Retty Rocker cried out as Billy Bonka just stood there casually. A-Aron ducked and dodged, slashing as he went. Various fruits came flying at him in a continuous wave. He pressed forward towards Billy Bonka with every step, closer and closer. With a mighty cry and powerful slash, A-Aron threw all his strength into a final swing, cutting through every fruit in his path and bursting others around the sword by the energy power radiating from it.

As A-Aron got closer to Billy Bonka, he turned his hat over, and immediately waves of never-ending hard candy fell out, with incredible speed the candy piled up around Billy Bonka. "Pure Imagination," Billy Bonka said, smiling as A-Aron's sword finally connected with him.

Swoosh! the sword went clean through the pile of the never-ending candy with Billy Bonka in the center. The pile of candy collapsed. Nothing was left inside. No sign of defeat or victory was seen or heard from A-Aron's attack. But Billy Bonka was gone.

Retty Rocker didn't waste time and began fighting A-Aron with her giant red spoon. They clashed, again and again, neither one making any ground. Lord Thomas still lay there, Retty seemed determined to ensure the deed was done and continued to attempt to strike him, and each time A-Aron would intercept and counter. They went on like this for some time.

Chapter 11

Explosions filled the air. A-Aron's toasted pastries were flying even as they fought sword to spoon. Retty wasn't giving up and while she would use her spoon to deflect A-Aron's sword, she launched a fruit snack strike, which came at A-Aron like a machine gun.

A-Aron then braced himself against the attack, grunting as he did. He took most of the force himself while trying to use his sword to block what he could. Retty Rocker let out a yell as she put all her strength into this attack to press harder. A-Aron wasn't going to last long. He kneeled and continued to brace against Retty's attack. Retty Rocker stepped forward as she continued her assault.

Suddenly, there was a surge of energy coming from A-Aron. The air was electrified, and fruit scent filled the air. A-Aron stood up, the attack Retty Rocker was using, deflected harmlessly off him. His eyes were white. A-Aron's sword was back down to regular size, but it was more powerful now.

'Level Up, New Abilities: Unlocked.'

"I have leveled up. You have lost," A-Aron said, his voice almost echoing as he spoke. 'High Jump,' A-Aron suddenly launched into the air with such force that the earth shook. He brought his sword down, yelling as he did. "Cleaver Chop!" A-Aron said as he fell, bringing his sword down in a chop motion onto Retty Rocker's position. She tried to dodge but couldn't. The energy from A-Aron's sword extended out as he hit the ground with it causing the ground to shake and cracks in the ground that shot right under where Retty stood.

'Hit,' Retty quickly jumped to one side of the growing space between the ground now but didn't have long to collect herself as A-Aron pushed in. Clash! Swoosh! A-Aron's sword met Retty's spoon as they fought, A-Aron pushing in and Retty trying her best just to hold her ground. After what seemed like several minutes, Retty found an opening and used it.

The sky darkened more than the usual it should be for the early evening it was by this time. Lightning hit the ground all over. A-Aron paused slightly to assess the situation. Before he could react, Retty Rocker's spoon had been replaced with two Fruity Feet whip strips of her own. But these were quite different from the ones Lord Thomas used. These were red, orange, and black. Sweet and fiery energy flavor swirled around; A-Aron stood ready. He didn't need to fear this anymore.

Retty cracked them fast and hard, breaking the ground as she did. A-Aron played defense at first and just blocked what he could to gauge how to attack. A-Aron relaunched his toasted pastry attack, as before, they materialized above him and shot out at his target. Retty dodged most and used her whips to block and counter.

Lightning was still striking the ground everywhere as they fought. Every time Retty Rocker would power up an attack, more lightning would hit the ground. When suddenly, as she pushed her power levels to the max, a huge bolt of lightning struck the land where Lord Thomas was lying yet. A-Aron quickly glanced over but couldn't see anything because of the flash of light. Retty used this moment of distraction to get him.

Crack! Retty snapped one of her whips around A-Aron's neck, pulling him to his knees. The whip in her left hand still swinging freely, taunting him.

"Just like it's supposed to be!" Retty said to A-Aron as he struggled to break free. "Big Media will be pleased with this." She continued as she pushed the electric shocks through the Fruity Feet whip strip connected to A-Aron's neck. She then whipped the Fruity Feet whip in her left hand over her head, and as she did so, it extended to a ridiculously long length. She drew it back to snap forward at A-Aron as she said, "You will always belong at the end of a…" Crack! The whip cracked forward, and A-Aron braced for impact, but it never came. Still struggling, he looked up at Retty, whose eyes were wide with fear! A-Aron's eyes followed her gaze until he saw it too. Her whip was caught and wrapped around the right forearm of, Lord Thomas.

"My man!" A-Aron shouted with excitement as best he could while still taking the whip's electric fruit shocks around his neck.

"Impossible," Retty Rocker cried, stuck, staring in disbelief.

I just stood there casual but tense, holding the whip around my arm; the fruit shocks just glancing off harmlessly. "Looks like you need to get with the times," I said as I pulled the whip tighter towards me.

Upon feeling the tension grow against her hand as I pulled the whip, she pushed a massive surge of energy down the whip in an attempt to break free. That plan backfired because as the power got to me, I quickly bounced it back at her sending Retty flying backward, releasing A-Aron from the whip in her right hand. In contrast, her left hand was torn away from the whip it was holding since it was wrapped around my arm as the energy pushed her back several yards. I threw the Fruity Feet whip down as I started to walk towards A-Aron.

A-Aron collected himself and stood up as I walked over to him, fruity scented, colorful shocks still randomly coursing over my clothes. "How?" A-Aron asked in disbelief, still catching his breath.

"My task," I started to reply as I looked at him, then corrected myself. "Our task is not yet done. Bigger forces are at work here that even I'm not fully aware of."

Retty Rocker was still struggling to get up from where she fell, coughing loudly. A-Aron and I glanced over to see where she was. As Retty got up slowly, A-Aron and I walked a little closer.

"You think you've won?" Retty exclaimed. "You! You and your precious friendship!"

"Don't end it this way," I responded. "Give us the info on Big Media and then leave here in exile, and you will at least have your life."

"Save your pity and your mercy!" Retty responded angrily. "I have no use for it." As she finished speaking, lightning struck her. Her energy level spiked; nothing changed on the outside. But A-Aron and I could feel the difference radiating off her.

"You will not survive a second time, my lord," Retty said cockily, adding that sarcasm to the title at the end.

"Don't underestimate us," I quickly pipped back. "And the proper title is. Fruit Ninja!" As I finished, I put my fists together in front of me and said, "Tootie Fruity powers activate!"

'Level up. Max level attained, Fruit Ninja Status: Active, New Abilities: Unlocked.' Instantly the air and energy built around me. I was suddenly dressed in traditional ninja clothes, except these were tie-dye colors; my mask was left down around my neck, electric shocks traveled around my clothes. My hair was back up in a ponytail, and my eyes glossed over in a solid color that changed every few seconds through every color of the rainbow.

"Are you ready?" I asked A-Aron.

"You know it!"

A sword materialized in my hand, like what I wielded before as we charged. Retty Rocker was ready and charged back. Red spoon in one hand and a Fruity Feet whip strip in the other. We clashed for a few moments, but the fight wouldn't last long. After a few exchanges, we paused, standing a few feet from each other, almost in a triangle shape.

"Together!" I yelled to A-Aron, and we swung our swords, slashing down on Retty's position.

Retty blocked but couldn't withstand us together now. Her power was weakening. Seconds after we hit her, there was a flash of light as lightning shot up to the sky. Afterward, A-Aron and I walked over to the smoking spot where Retty Rocker was. Nothing was left but a pile of what looked like frosting, but it moved weird, on its own, like a consciously aware sludge. A-Aron knelt to inspect it and touched it with a fingertip.

"Just regular frosting," he said as he brought the sample up to his face and smelled it. As he wiped off his finger and energy came from the pile and connected with the piece in his hand! A-Aron was frozen stiff. I tried to help him, but it was too late; the energy transference had already locked him in.

It only lasted a minute or two before A-Aron was back to normal, and the energy stopped. The frosting melted into the ground, and A-Aron fell to one knee breathing heavily.

"Are you okay?" I asked earnestly.

"I'm better than okay," he replied. "I realized why Retty Rocker was afraid of me and what I'd become if she didn't have me destroyed."

"What's that?"

"Culinary Master, and a Fruit Ninja."

"No way!" I exclaimed.

"I have ascended."

'Level up. Max level attained, Fruit Ninja Status: Active, New Abilities: Unlocked.' The messages scrolled past A-Aron's face. To show what he knew, A-Aron put his fists together in front of him as I did before, "Tootie Fruity powers activate." Immediately his clothes changed to match mine with one small difference. Instead of tie-dye colors and patterns, his ninja clothes were zebra-striped with multiple colors. His eyes matched mine with bright solid colors that filled the whole eye and changed every few seconds alternating between the rainbow colors.

"This is awesome!" I exclaimed.

"Right?"

We both just stood for a few moments. The smell of fruit was strong in the air. The sun was setting; the fields were torn apart from the battles that had just ensued.

"We need to find out more about Big Media and what their or its agenda is," I said.

"I agree."

And with that, we powered down and began to walk back to town. We were done, for now. Hopefully.

Chapter 12

A-Aron and I spent the next few months trying to live a low-key life while still seeking out Big Media and their agenda. We appeared normal in dress and appearance unless we activated the Fruit Ninja powers. We were only bringing it out when the situation called for it. We usually tried to stick to the shadows, secretly hitting targets that we hoped would bring us closer to our prize. However, regardless of who we talked to or what we found, every trail ended, and every lead proved useless.

A few months later, A-Aron and I were following up on a lead from an anonymous source about some beings that have been shifting in and out of our realm that we needed to address, signed only 'P.L.' It was a most curious note since we hadn't widely exposed ourselves as the Fruit Ninjas.

Still, we felt we should at least check it out. Perhaps we might find a clue to finally get closer to solving the mystery of Big Media and its influence over our lands. During our trek into the forest between our realm and the next, we searched for any sign of something that was trying to invade through here.

"Anything?" I asked A-Aron as we met up in the clearing towards the center of the woods.

"Nothing."

Then we saw it. A figure approached from the opposite edge of the clearing. He wore red and black type clothing, a red braided cape, and a strange hat with a twisted red cane.

His overall appearance was that of a man of ancient royalty.

"Who are you?" A-Aron asked as the man stopped a few yards away from us.

"And what do you want?" I added.

"I am the Lord of the Licorice Laces," he said as he bowed to us. "And I have come to claim this land as part of my own."

"Sorry," I said, "but this realm is taken."

"If you don't leave," A-Aron quickly added, "this realm is protected, and you will meet your end here."

"Protected?" asked the man. The puzzled look on his face seemed to indicate that he was genuinely surprised by this news. "That wasn't what I was told," he muttered softly under his breath.

"Told?" A-Aron repeated as we glanced at each other with puzzled looks.

"What do you mean, told?" I asked, turning back to the Licorice Lord.

"Well, no matter," the lord responded to himself, ignoring my question.

"Who is this protector?" he then asked us directly.

"Us!" A-Aron and I replied in unison.

"Fine then!" the Lord of Licorice responded, tapping his twisted cane on the ground. Long licorice ropes started to come out of the ground around him. An evil smile on his face appeared. "Let's see how good you are."

"Time to send your ass back to your own land of candy!" I shouted as I pointed at him menacingly.

"It's ninja time!" A-Aron and I shouted together. "Tootie Fruity powers activate!" we said as we put our fists together in front of us as before.

As we started forward, a bright light shone, our clothes changed as we walked, the tie-dye and colored zebra prints as before, our eyes changed flashing colors of the rainbow. In unison, we both reached back over our shoulders and drew our swords. Glancing at each other, nodding in affirmative. We charged the intruder…

…And so we fought. Defending the realm from all kinds of monsters. We never forgot our primary mission; the search for Big Media and to be rid of its influence. But we would not let our realm be taken in the meantime, not while we had the power to stop it.

The power of magic… the power of friendship… The secret warriors… The Fruit Ninjas!

Epilogue

Silent whispers of the wind were all you heard. The temple at the top of the Dragon Mountain remained empty as it always had. Empty, save for one jellybean. In the middle of the floor. The wind blew through the temple, whistling and echoing as it did. Then, ever so faint, you could hear through the air. Singing. Soft at first but getting louder and more apparent.

"If you come with me, you will be," the voice trailed off as it often did. A brown top hat appeared in the center of the floor, covering the jellybean. Footsteps approached; a figure picked up the hat. You could hear a whistle as the footsteps got softer as they walked away before he vanished completely.

The same figure from the temple suddenly appeared at the shore of the boiling gelatin lake in the center of the mountain. Without spells or assistance, the man walked over the gelatin and into the cave on the island at the center. The fruit smell that was there when Lord Thomas came through was gone. A humid rank air of hot chocolate was all you could smell now. The center of the cave had a caged cell. In the cage was a man; a short man in royal garb, peppermint swirls around his shoulders and on the stockings he wore. Gingerbread scales for armor, but no shoes, no crown. He sat in the cage, depressed and lonely.

"You'd be free from here and at least have your kingdom if you'd do what they ask," said the figure to the caged man through the bars.

"I will never help the likes of them," came the soft but firm reply from the prisoner.

"As you wish," the figure replied. "But I should warn you; we always get what we want." The man continued more menacingly as he grabbed the bars and brought his face closer. "Candy King," he finished mockingly.

The Secrets of Bastien Manor
(A Horror Story)

For my daughter Arwen. Who specifically requested a scary story she could read.

Chapter 1

The stagecoach was bouncing rather uncomfortably. It was a long road out to the Manor and Draven was lost in his thoughts. It would be no easy nor restful trip, however. Thunder cracked; a flash of lightning was seen briefly illuminating the landscape. Not that there was much to see beyond the woods. Why anyone would want to live this far out away from the city was beyond any thought Draven could imagine.

No rain, Draven thought to himself as he stared out the window. It was a strange thing to witness. With as much thunder and lightning as there was, you'd expect it to be a complete storm. Even more peculiar was that it seemed to come out of nowhere. His trek from the city was quiet, and nightfall was approaching. The moon was shining bright that evening. That is, until it suddenly wasn't. This added to the uneasiness of his nerves, which were already heightened because of the nature of the trip.

Lord Bastien was a known recluse but a nobleman who liked to stay in retreat at his Manor just outside the forest on the other side of the city. It was no common feat to head out this way at a half a day's ride from almost any civilization. Perhaps that's what Lord Bastien was going for? Draven only knew him from a few of the social interactions that the Lord would partake in within the city limits. To his recollection, no one that he knew had ever been to the Manor, much less received an invite to go there. But he stated that it was of utmost importance and urgency.

More thunder and lightning crashed. Draven could hear the horse and driver outside his carriage growing restless. Typically, he would've made a protest about the ride, but not this time. He couldn't fault them, not tonight. Besides, it was no small fee to get the driver to agree to take him all the way. Rumors, of course, spread of the secrets within the Manor and of the monster of Lord Bastien. These were, of course, just rumors spread from the common rabble in the taverns and other less than savory places. Those people liked their scary stories and twisted tales. It helped distract them from their already unpleasant lives.

The stagecoach pulled up around the corner, exiting the woods. Draven looked out and saw the shadowy silhouette of the Manor. It was hard to make out entirely, though, given the cloud cover that night. Draven could see faint lights in some of the windows of the Manor and a few outside lights along the drive up to the house.

It was a strange sight, as if the lights were straining to light up more than they could, almost as if something was suppressing the light, keeping it dim and barely lit. As they got through the gate and on the house drive, a flash of lightning lit up the sky. For a brief moment, Draven could see the house in full, three stories tall with two towers extending another beyond that in height.

The carriage stopped just at the bottom of the stairs. Draven stepped out and took a deep breath to help calm his nerves. He couldn't speculate on the nature of the visit, nor could he assume any detail since he felt like a stranger to Lord Bastien. Draven looked up at the house, thunder pounded, and lightning cracked again. Strange, he thought as he observed the flash. It almost seemed that the lightning shot out of the roof of the Manor. Draven shook his head and chalked it up to his eyes, playing tricks. Lightning was known to strike houses. Seeing it up close was no surprise to him. But, to see it shoot out of the roof, connecting with the clouds – that seemed the more problematic. Which, considering the circumstances, made it that much worse for the nerves this evening.

Draven climbed the stone stairs up to the front door. The staircase was elaborate and wide enough for three to four people to walk side by side with ease. The front doors were double doors, which opened inward. Each one was wooden and taller than the average door. They had a light on each side. Like the others, it was very dim. As if they too were straining to shine as bright as they should be. Draven got to the doors and paused momentarily. As he reached up to grab the knocker mounted on the outside of the door, they opened. As if someone was watching and triggered an automatic response, both doors glided open effortlessly and surprisingly, with no noise.

Draven took a moment to collect himself as he stepped into the entryway. As he got past the front entrance, the doors swung shut behind him, only sounding when they clicked together. Draven whirled around at this moment, staring puzzled at the doors. "Your coat, sir," a pale voice muttered from the side. Draven shot a startled glance towards the voice. His muscles tensed, and he stood slightly defensive. "Apologizes for the startle, sir. But if you could give me your coat, I'll hang it in the closet," the man finished.

Draven calmed down as the figure who spoke stepped

into the dim light of the entry. An older gentleman, balding and frail looking. He was dressed in standard servant attire and held out an empty hand, waiting to receive what he had asked for. "Oh, yes. Of course," Draven finally said, taking off his coat. Draven then gave it to the butler. The butler stepped forward quickly and grabbed the coat with a strength that surprised Draven, given the sight of the older man.

"Lord Bastien and the other guests are waiting for you in the library," the butler said as he folded the coat and turned to walk away. "Through the foyer on the left under the stairs," he said as he walked away from Draven. He disappeared into the blackness that was the joining room on Draven's right.

Others, Draven thought. The invite said nothing nor inclined any hint of the possibility of other guests. Although, given the strange nature of the invite, he shouldn't be assuming anything about this meeting. Looking ahead, Draven noticed the staircase on his left going up, a few small lights on the railing to light up the way. The stairs were almost as wide as the front steps and some type of polished stone or marble. The upstairs was dark, and though it would appear that the lights on the top of the stairs should illuminate the upper balcony looking down to the foyer where Draven stood, they did not. It was as if some dark curtain was dark, keeping the light from hitting anything but what it was allowed to.

Immediately to his right was the darkroom the butler disappeared in. No door was in this room, just a large archway. Similarly, like the staircase outside, the darkness within seemed only to be blocked by the small lights in the entryway. But even they seemed to stop right at the entrance of this area. Further down on his right was another oversized door, where it led was left to mystery since it, like all the others, was closed. Three other doors, two more directly ahead and the one on the left, under the stairs. All were closed save this one. A soft light came from the doorway as Draven walked closer.

Reaching the entrance of the doorway under the stairs, he heard a few muffled voices. Feeling a sense of calm again as he realized he wasn't alone, Draven entered with a slight pip in his step, the kind of pip that he would use at any one of the formal gatherings that he was familiar with in the past. This occasion, however, had kept him less than himself. He hoped that with the presence of others like himself here, he would feel more at ease about the place.

As he entered the library, Draven noticed first the vast collection of books on display. The library was no exaggeration. Every wall, floor to ceiling, had bookshelves full of books of every size and shape. Turning to his right in the middle of the room, there was a couch and a few sitting chairs. These were located close to the fireplace, the only spot on the walls that had no books. End tables were placed decoratively throughout, and lamps on most of them. In the far end of the room, near the only window, was a large desk. Draven thought for a moment about how big everything was here compared to other houses he'd seen.

Behind the desk was an oversized chair that any man could be surrounded by when seated. The window had open curtains, but all that was seen was the reflection of the objects in the room. Sitting on the couch were three people of some high social standing based on their clothes. Two women and a man. The first woman on the left, slim and angular. She held a long cigarette in her right hand and, in her left, a drink of some kind in a fancy glass. Her eyes pierced Draven as he met hers as he entered. She wore a simple yet elegant dress and matching hat, her hair was done up behind her head, and she was adorned with a heavily jeweled necklace.

Next was the man; he was also well dressed in a traditional black dinner jacket. A thick mustache was on his upper lip, and a fat cigar was in his mouth. He was of average height and build, with just a bit of extra plumpness forming around his midsection. He seemed unfazed by Draven's entrance and merely glanced back down at the book he was reading. There was another woman on Draven's right, sitting at the end of the couch closest to the fire. At first glance, she was much younger than the other and very pretty. She wore a muffled green dress and no jewelry save for a single gem in her headband, a fiery green emerald that accented her dress well. Her hair was down loose and reached just past her shoulders.

Another man was present, standing opposite the trio with his back to Draven's position. He didn't acknowledge Draven's entrance at first but continued speaking in a hushed tone that Draven couldn't make out from where he stood. Catching the gaze of the people on the couch, the man turned to face the new arrival. "Welcome, Draven," the man said plainly. A smile formed on his lips, but there was no excitement nor happiness in his greeting.

Draven bowed his head simply in response. "Lord Bastien."

"May I introduce the Lady Elizabeth," Lord Bastien said, gesturing to the woman on the far end of the couch. Draven nodded, and the woman, never taking her eyes off Draven, instead, merely lifted her glass and tipped her head slightly and smiled coyly. "The Duke of Hutchinson," Bastien continued as he gestured to the man seated in the middle. Draven nodded again. The Duke set down his book and leaned forward slightly to bow in return without leaving his seat. "And finally, the lovely, Miss Anne," Bastien finished. Draven nodded a third time in greeting. Miss Anne stood and gave a more formal curtsy, much to the disdain of the Lady Elizabeth, who had a superiority complex about her.

"You've already met my butler, Charlie," Lord Bastien said, directing his gaze to the back of the room. Draven's heart jumped in his throat. The pale, frail man that greeted him at the door was at the back of the room, partially hidden in shadow. How? Draven thought quickly, there was no other door, and no one walked past him entering the room. There must be another door at the other end he had not seen in the dark there. Yes. That was the only explanation. The butler stepped forward more into the light and bowed low as a servant would.

Draven took a few steps closer after calming down. "Good evening to you all." Then turning to Lord Bastien, he asked, "Is everything all right? Your letter sounded urgent."

"I'm not sure," the Lord replied, glancing back into the fire. He was an older man but spoke like someone who may be younger. He was well built and fit, but his skin always looked a little sickly. Draven waited before speaking again. Lord Bastien snapped out of his thoughts, walked to the drink table, and poured something into a glass. Picking up the glass and walking over to Draven, he handed it to him and told him to sit.

Draven did as he was told, almost forcefully. Like, he didn't really want to sit, but he couldn't help himself and must. Lord Bastien's voice was rich yet smooth. The thunder pounded outside loudly. Draven glanced up at the ceiling as if to be inspecting it after the sound. "Spooky night," he said as he sipped his drink. Turning to the others seated across from him. "How do you know Lord Bastien?" None of them answered but merely looked at him, almost ashamed that he would ask such a thing. Draven didn't let them see how that bothered him – turning to Lord Bastien, who was on his right now, standing in front of the fire again.

"I'm going to die soon," Bastien finally said smoothly.

Chapter 2

Die! Draven couldn't help but cringe at the thought. "What do you mean?" he asked. Lord Bastien didn't budge. The others still sitting across from Draven on the couch only showed slight shock in their faces. Draven now moved forward in his seat and grew tense. "What do you mean?" he repeated earnestly. The thunder sounded again, and the lightning cracked. Lord Bastien turned to face the group at the same time as the lightning flashed. The light flashed through the window and reflected off the Lord's face. His angular features were pronounced for a moment. Draven wasn't sure what to think, but he refused to sit back and do nothing. Answers were needed.

"I'm going to die soon," Bastien repeated, though this time more solemnly. "I've invited you all here because you are the most capable of helping me with this." Bastien shifted as he spoke, standing in front of the fire facing them fully.

Draven sat back in his chair and thought hard. The three others across from him seemed to do the same. No doubt the same question was on everyone's mind at this point. How can we stop it? And how does he know he will die? "And what are we to do about it, and why should we care? We hardly know you," the Lady Elizabeth snorted. Draven shot a questioning glance at her. It was the sort of thing that would come from her mouth, given the very little Draven knew about her thus far. So he was not surprised that she said it, and as correct as it may have been, there were – more polite ways to say it.

It seemed that Draven was not alone as the others murmured in agreement with Lady Elizabeth's words. They seemed to know Lord Bastien about as well as he did. Almost on cue with that thought, Lord Bastien answered, "I know that you don't know me that well. And you all don't know each other." He was pacing casually as he spoke. "But you know me better than any other would, and you will come to know each other well enough in your stay here."

"Wait. We are staying here?" Lady Elizabeth snapped.

"Yes," Lord Bastien said casually. "You'll all stay here until we figure out what in this house is trying to kill me. You've all been selected to assist based on our previous engagements. I can trust no one else for this mystery."

Lord Bastien's words were smooth. There was little push back save for a thought by Draven about clothing and notifying family about the extended stay. But before he could speak, again, Lord Bastien was already answering his concern. "I've already had your drivers return to town with letters informing your houses of your intended stay." He straightened up slightly as he paused. Draven almost felt like his presence grew. More domineering, more forceful. "They will be summoned again when we finish, you each have been assigned a room, and you'll find clothes a-plenty that should suit your tastes," Lord Bastien finished.

Draven sat rather uncomfortably, Lord Bastien's words again were smooth and firm, but Draven had a question. "If this house is trying to kill you, should we not also be worried for our own lives? Why not just leave? Surely this is a matter for the police."

"No," Lord Bastien was quick to answer. His demeanor

stiffened at first but softened immediately. "No," he repeated. "This house is all I have and must keep it... I have to keep it. It won't let me go, and if any major intervention were to happen, it would surely be catastrophic." Bastien glanced around the room as he finished, searching for something hidden in the walls. Like he knew something was there but didn't know where to look.

Draven sat puzzled, following the gaze of Lord Bastien around the room. "What should we be looking for? And where should we start?" he asked. Not sure why, however, the question came out of Draven's mouth, but his brain didn't lead to those questions. Was something in the house? Draven could tell something was off about the whole thing. But what, precisely, still eluded his grasp. His logical mind fought such notions of superstition. If something were here, there would be a logical explanation.

The other three seemed to agree with Draven's questions. Each one shifted in their seat and looked at Lord Bastien for the answers. Bastien just stood still, looking down at each guest. "I don't know what we'll find, and I don't know where or how to find it. But perhaps we should start first thing tomorrow? After we all get a good night's sleep."

The Lady Elizabeth let out a soft retort. "I doubt that will happen here," she remarked. As she stood up, she continued and said, "But if you'll excuse me then, I'll go turn in for the night. We can play detective in the morning." The others agreed and got up to follow her. Lord Bastien beckoned to Charlie to take them up to their rooms.

Draven got up with everyone else and proceeded to be escorted to the bedrooms. He noticed that, despite the initial disdain mentioned by Lady Elizabeth, they all, including himself, felt no need to push back. As if they had all known each other forever and agreed to help of their own volition. Draven couldn't speak for the others, but as he joined them in following the butler to the stairs, he could tell something wasn't quite right. Draven wanted to leave, but he felt like staying. He didn't care, but he did.

Reaching the stairs, Draven took up the rear and looked beyond the group to the top of the stairs. The dark curtain that was there when he arrived was somewhat less now. The lights on the stairs seemed to brighten as they ascended. Reaching the top, the balcony was then lit by more than just the top staircase light. Other wall lights spaced sporadically around the entry and down the hall. Draven assumed there must've been a gas switch downstairs that Lord Bastien opened, knowing they were headed this way.

The group followed the butler as he led each to their rooms. The house didn't have many bedrooms, but after seeing Miss Anne take the first one, Draven knew why. The room was huge, with a full upholstered bed, a walk-in closet, and a seating area with a fireplace. The room also had a bathroom within it. As they moved to each room, Draven noticed it was the same. Each room was mirrored off the others and with identical furniture set up.

Draven's room was on the end of the hall towards the back of the Manor. The butler was more beside him now rather than in front. Draven thought about making small talk but decided against it. HHHSSSSS, a soft hiss like whisper came from above. Draven shot a glance up and paused. The butler stopped and turned to look at Draven with curiosity. Draven was frozen still. He couldn't see the ceiling through the dark. The darkness-like curtain was thick, the lights on the wall stopped short a small distance from the top of the doorways. Beyond that, nothing.

"Are you all right, sir?" Charlie finally asked. This question broke Draven's thought, and he looked at the butler but said nothing. "It's quite normal, sir," the butler said as if reading Draven's thoughts. "The ceiling is quite high, and the wind sometimes catches the roof just right."

Once in his room, Draven checked the closet first. Sure enough, several outfits were Draven's size, as well as sleep attire. Strange, he thought. How did Lord Bastien know what to keep here? If each guest was selected, when did he find out their clothing size, and how long had this visit been planned?

Entering the bathroom, he noticed it was slightly behind the modern plumbing. The bath had a drain, but no means to get water, and the toilet was a crude seat with a tank of water mounted on the wall above it. The tank had a pipe running up through the ceiling, no doubt to a larger tank on the roof that was used to refill the toilet tank. After changing into his nighttime attire, Draven grabbed a book from the small bookcase near the fireplace and sat down to read. The fire was burning well and combined with the light from the bed lamp Draven was feeling better and more comfortable. The thunder outside had gotten softer, and the lightning flashed less as if the storm was passing. Draven didn't bother to go to the window to check, partly from nerves, partly from a lack of curiosity.

As comfortable as Draven felt, he still had difficulty falling asleep as he settled into bed sometime later. Lord Bastien's words played again in his mind. I'm going to die soon. What a strange way to put it. We will all die soon, soon being relative to each person's lifespan. But if it's a known doom incoming, most would seek to avoid it, not drive straight for it.

Draven must have fallen asleep at some point since he awoke sometime later that night to a strange scratching sound outside his door. He lit a candle and very carefully opened his bedroom door. Peering into the hallway, Draven looked around cautiously. The lights were still lit, though much dimmer than before, barely giving any light beyond the lamps that held them on the walls. Draven stepped out and looked up and down the hallway. Seeing nothing, he decided to walk the hall and find out if the noise came from another guest.

Scratch, Scratch, Scratch! Like claws on the wood. It was moving quickly across the walls. Draven turned quickly and looked. Nothing. The sounds stopped almost as fast as they started. Draven turned back to continue walking down the hall away from his room. His nerves were tense, and though Draven tried to explain what he heard to himself, it didn't help him calm down.

He reached the first room that was closest to his, the Duke's room. Draven took a deep breath and went to knock on the door. He paused before his hand connected with the door. There was probably no need to wake the others for random sounds heard. There appeared to be no real threat, and as the butler stated before, the wind makes all kinds of noises in this house.

Draven decided to walk to the balcony, the lights were still very dim on the walls, and his candle wasn't much additional help. Barely lighting up the floor before him, Draven carefully and slowly walked down the hall towards the stairs. As the hallway widened out on the balcony connecting to the stairs, Draven noticed that the lights downstairs were dimmed as well, though there was something heavier in the dark down there. Something different. As he approached the railing overlooking the front entryway, Draven held out his candle to help illuminate the floor below. Not much good it did. The candle was almost snuffed out by the thick darkness that filled the air below him.

Not much to see, save for the few small dots of light where the lamps on the walls near the door were. Scratch, Scratch, Scratch! Draven whirled around to look behind him. He moved so quickly out of fright that he almost caused his candle to extinguish. Glancing around quickly, using his hand to block the wind and protect his candlelight flame as he moved. Nothing. No creature nor person was seen or heard again.

Draven was about to calm down when, suddenly, he felt a tickle on the back of his neck. Taking a few steps back toward the hall, Draven then turned back to the railing on the balcony. Then he saw it, a red glow in the darkness above him. He stepped back and gasped. The light broke into two and grew brighter like two eyes peering through the fog of night at him. The darkness began to move. Swirls of smoke, it looked like, twisting into little tornados. Draven stumbled backward as the fear took over, he tried to call out, but no sound came from his mouth.

Draven fell to the floor, crawling away backward at his best as his gaze continued to be fixed on the eyes in the ceiling. Suddenly, he stopped moving; glancing back, Draven realized that he had hit the wall. Now cowered against the base of the wall, he sat in fear. He had lost his candle in his attempt to flee. The lights in the hallway brightened, though the darkness was still keeping them at bay. The eyes glowed brighter as he sat there, and they continued to grow brighter as the event unfolded.

Then, suddenly the smoke turned into bats. They were flying around screeching in their awful noise. Draven tried to yell as he covered his head. The bats flew around him, several hitting him in the process. Then, as if guided by some unknown force, they swarmed above, circling a few times then flying at an unnatural fast speed down the hallway. As Draven peered through his arms, still covering his head, he saw the doors of the other guests open. Each one walked out. He held up his hand in an attempt to warn them to stay inside their rooms. It was too late. The bats broke off and flew into every room above the heads of the other guests as they exited.

They didn't seem fazed by the ordeal. And after a moment, Draven knew why. Miss Anne limped out. Her body looked like rotting flesh, stumbling as she walked, her clothes tattered and torn. Bugs of all kinds fell out of the holes in her skin at various places. Her eyes were gone; only dark hollow sockets remained. Lady Elizabeth was more normal looking, though pale and sickly. She walked casually in Draven's direction approaching Miss Anne's side; she then promptly smiled and then removed her head, tearing it off the collar. Her face didn't change; the body simply held it down at her side.

Simultaneously, the Duke stumbled in his way, gripping his neck as blood poured out. As he reached the others, he held out the hand that was covering the wound – blood shot out, covering the ladies next to him. The Duke held out his hand as if offering aid to Draven. Draven looked up. The Duke's face was yellowing, his teeth looked half rotten, and his breath reeked of death. Draven slapped the hand away. As he did so, it broke off at the wrist, like some snap-on accessory. The Duke bellowed in pain as he stood back up, clutching the arm of the broken appendage.

Draven pushed back harder against the wall. The darkness was still swirling overhead; the bats continued to fly in the manner they had been. The sounds of the bats, the Duke's cry and now a deep rolling laugh was heard. Draven looked up, the bats stopped, turning back into the smoky darkness, swirling around again. But this time, it grew more intense. The other guests inched forward; the Duke's hand was flopping on its own near Draven's feet. He kicked it away. The hand flew away and was consumed by the encroaching darkness. It moved in from all sides; one by one, the others were lost in it, the red eyes above grew brighter with each piece taken in by the shadows.

Draven tried again to call out, to yell some kind of plea for help. Still no sound was made. The darkness moved in closer around him. The eyes glowed brighter and moved in closer, or were they getting bigger? Draven couldn't tell. He felt his way in panic along the edge of the hallway, trying to get to his room. The eyes followed as he went. The darkness was now upon him; Draven could feel it. A sudden cold chill on his skin where the darkness was beginning to creep in.

Draven felt it in his legs first, wrapping around them as it went up to his back and chest. Still trying to scream, but to no avail. Like fingers reaching up over his shoulders, Draven quickened his pace. He couldn't see anything in front of him, the red eyes glowed above, and the darkness howled around as he crawled. Draven felt a stinging sensation as the darkness reached to encompass his head. He got up off his hands as if he was being pulled back by his hair. His arms stiff, his voice lost. The darkness crept over his face. Draven's eyes filled with fear as the shadowy fingers suddenly penetrated his ears, eyes and mouth. Draven screamed loud, partially from fear, partially from pain. Still no sound was heard, and for what seemed like an eternity, he was frozen.

Then, he tried to scream again. The darkness was all around him now. He could feel it, swallowing him up bit by bit. Suddenly, for no reason, his voice was free and loud. "HEEELLLPPPP!" was heard.

Then it all went black.

Chapter 3

Draven shot up out of his bed. His scream still echoed in his throat. Frantically, he felt all around himself to confirm if the previous night's events were real. He glanced around his room. Light was seen around the edges of his curtains. Draven breathed a massive sigh of relief as he took a deep breath to calm down.

Draven carefully got up and opened the drapes. The sunlight hit everything with a stark shine. Draven squinted as his eyes adjusted to the light. Once his eyes cleared, Draven looked around the room. Nothing changed. Everything was in its place. Draven was sure it had been a dream, nothing more, and with this idea, he promptly got himself washed and presentable for the day.

He did wonder how his dream played out to the others. Draven heard himself yelling as he woke up, he could still recall all the details, and he remembered trying to call out a few times. Though he couldn't speak in his dream, he wondered if the others could hear him calling out in his sleep. Draven decided that he wouldn't bring it up unless they asked. Remembering the size of the rooms and the distance between them it was doubtful that the others heard him. If he did, in fact, actually call out in his sleep because of the dream.

Exiting his room, Draven noticed that other rooms were empty, and the doors were open. The others must already be awake and elsewhere. Glancing around casually as he walked, he got to the balcony and turned to look up and around where he stood. Memories of last night still played in his head, though now in the morning light, it all seemed less intense and fearful.

The lamps were still dimly lit; however, the light from the giant window above the front doors overpowered the artificial light within the Manor. Draven used this to his advantage and inspected the walls and floor where he remembered crouching. His candle was still in his room on the bed stand, and there was no sign of wax or remnants of where he had dropped it last night.

This, combined with the ability to see the ceiling in the hallway, calmed Draven's nerves and convinced him that nothing that happened last night was real. The ceiling was higher than most in the hallway but not as high as the roof over the entryway, which appeared to be a vaulted ceiling connecting straight to the roof. There were a couple of other doors on the balcony near the hallway. Draven made a point to remember these and investigate further. For now, however, breakfast. A little fear and mystery shouldn't be the reason to ruin one's routine nor their appetite.

Once Draven reached the main floor, he heard some soft voices through the archway where the butler had taken his coat the night before. Light from the window lit up the room so Draven could see clearly, unlike the night prior. Entering the room, he noticed a few cabinets holding dishes and various kitchen items. In the corner was a closet that still had the door open. Inside were several coats and outer garments. One of which was Draven's. Good to know, Draven thought. It will be handy to know where he could find that should he need it later.

Through the other side of the room was a standard-size doorway that led into a parlor room. Here, the other guests were sitting comfortably around the breakfast table, each enjoying a different dish. The light from the window here made Draven feel the most comfortable. The room was smaller but had a brighter feel with the white furniture, floral wallpaper, and smell of food.

Draven approached the empty chair at the table and exchanged greetings with the others. "Have you seen Charlie yet?" the Duke asked.

"No. I haven't," Draven replied. "Should I have?"

Before the Duke could answer, Lady Elizabeth cut in, "He's probably still in the kitchen. It's taking longer than it should to make my eggs," she said distastefully as she sipped on her coffee.

Draven ignored her and turned to ask the Duke where the kitchen was. The Duke just nodded as he took a bite of his food. As Draven got up, the Lady Elizabeth just shot him a smug look. "Tell him to hurry with my eggs."

Draven only smiled in response. He glanced at Miss Anne. She was slowly picking at her food, and their eyes met briefly. Draven didn't need but a moment to understand. Her night was just as terrifying as his was. The fear and uncertainty were still lingering in her eyes. Draven headed across the room to the kitchen. *Was it possible that we all had the same dream?* he thought. Though it was improbable, Draven decided that he would inquire about it when the opportunity presented itself. Perhaps the Duke and the Lady had similar nights.

Following the smell of food, Draven headed through the doorway on the far side of the room. Inside was a very large, ancient-style kitchen: stone floor, with a large stone fireplace that doubled as an oven. In the center of the room was a large table full of random ingredients and food products – Wash bins and a drying rack on the opposite wall, pot and pans hanging from the ceiling. Charlie was just coming in from outside carrying a handful of eggs.

"Good morning, sir," Charlie said in what Draven could only hope was a cheerful tone.

Draven bowed in response. "Good morning, Charlie," he said as he stepped down into the room. "The Duke was asking for you." Charlie rolled his eyes so slightly, Draven almost missed it.

"And you, sir?" Charlie asked as he began to chop some vegetables.

"Just curious about my breakfast options," Draven said politely, not wanting to be rude.

"Whatever you like," Charlie said without looking up from the table.

"Whatever you make will be fine," Draven said as he went up the few steps to exit the room.

"Excellent, sir."

As Draven approached the table where the other guests sat, he thought about asking them how their night was. He needed information about what the others were thinking without letting on precisely what happened to him – no need to have the rumors going around that he was crazy. As Draven sat down in his seat, the others barely acknowledged him. Draven was about to protest their behavior until he noticed it wasn't just him they ignored, but each other as well. Each person was just eating as if they were the only person there.

"So," Draven began. "How was your night?" The three others stirred uncomfortably in their seats.

The Lady Elizabeth was first to speak. "Just fine, considering the conditions." Miss. Anne nodded the same, and the Duke just winked at Draven while still chewing his mouthful of food. Before Draven could continue, Charlie came through the door bringing food. In front of Draven, he set a bowl of soup, eggs and toast. Then he set down a plate of some fruit pastries in front of the Duke, who, with much pleasure, quickly began to devour them. No doubt the reason for the Duke's interest in Charlie's whereabouts earlier was connected to the expected plate of food.

"Charlie," Draven said before the butler left the table.

"Yes, sir," Charlie replied. He stood very still and rigid as if he was suddenly snapped up straight at attention.

"Where is Lord Bastien this morning? I'm eager to speak with him about the events of last night," Draven finished as he sipped his tea while waiting for the butler to respond.

"Lord Bastien is indisposed this morning and will join you later," Charlie stated calmly. "He doesn't sleep much at night anymore and uses the morning hours to catch up on that sleep. Feel free to roam the grounds and the house." He finished and turned to walk away, but as he reached the doorway to the kitchen, he turned back. "Except for the east tower, that is where Lord Bastien resides, and you shouldn't disturb him. And as for your concerns about last night, you needn't worry. All will be revealed in good time." And with that, he vanished into the kitchen.

Draven was lost in thought. Did Charlie know about what happened in his dream? Or was it mere chance that he had the dream and Charlie referred to the conversation with Lord Bastien before bed? Not enough evidence for any conclusion to be made yet. However, he would note it for later. The others seemed curious about the butler's message, but no one initiated the conversation. So, Draven just let it go. More than likely, the answers would be found in their search of the house today.

The group began eating, and Draven stirred his soup. Two red vegetables floated in the broth. Draven's eyes fixated on the swirl of the broth for a moment as his thoughts went to last night. Suddenly the feeling of the dark on his skin was brought back. The immobilizing terror had Draven frozen in place until suddenly the two red vegetables became the shape of the red eyes seen in the darkness of the ceiling in his dream. As quickly as the eyes formed, they jumped out of the soup at Draven's face.

His trance was broken, and he snapped awake, nearly knocking over his teacup. The startled movement caused a slight fright in the trio with him. Draven quickly collected himself and excused his behavior. The others seemed less convinced but continued as they were.

Once breakfast was finished, the group headed to the library to discuss a plan of action.

"I think we should just let whatever happens happen," Lady Elizabeth sharply stated as she lit a cigarette while standing near the fireplace. The others and Draven were standing sporadically around the room but remained silent.

Miss Anne looked at some books on the wall near the far end of the room when she stopped suddenly and said, "I don't think that is a good idea." The group shifted to look in her direction as she continued, "Considering the dream I had last night." Draven's heart about jumped out of his chest. She had a dream too? He must know more. He didn't hide his facial expressions very well. Miss Anne immediately directed her gaze at him. "You had one too, didn't you?" she asked softly. Draven could only nod in response.

The Duke and the Lady Elizabeth both nodded to each other as well, and the group came in closer to each other as they shared the details of the night prior. Each dream was relatively similar, with some slight differences in the appearance of the other guests. But the eyes and the feeling of the darkness taking over, that was the same in every dream.

Chapter 4

From there, the group decided to walk the grounds first. Partially as a courtesy to the yet sleeping host and partly as a need to get out of the house and into the sunlight. While the house had a few windows scattered throughout, the light from outside barely lit up the rooms. Despite the morning sun, the house still held a very dreary feeling, almost life draining.

Getting outside, the group noticed a very elaborate garden out the back of the house. However, the garden was dead, yet it held its form and shape. The paths had scattered dead leaves about them, and the shrubs along the path were sickly looking, yet, still trimmed to their rigid flat top and sides shape.

The flower beds were weeded, but each plant left was barely clinging to life. Even the sun could not restore them to their full colorful bloom anymore. Street lanterns were spaced every so often around the garden, which, under any other circumstance, Draven thought would be nice to have for those late evening strolls. The fountain in the middle of the garden had water, but the water was still. The inside was clean; no leaves or grime was seen anywhere. Draven wondered how such work was done regularly, given the state of Charlie's physical ability.

The group split up a bit as they wandered around the garden area near the house. Draven walked out a bit and looked back up at home. Vines had taken over and covered the backside of the place where they were. Draven was more interested in architecture. He was hoping to see how the house's layout from the outside was compared to the inside.

From the outside, it was difficult to tell the exact layout of the interior without further exploration of the inside and checking the windows to match the rooms. Draven noticed the sun was receding behind the clouds coming in. As he continued to scan the house, he noticed a figure in the tower nearest him. He paused and looked harder. Unlike the far tower, this one was open, with just a few pillars around the outside edge to hold up the roof over it. But there was no railing, and no stairs were seen leading up to it. Must be a trap door in the floor, he thought.

Draven blinked once, and the figure he thought he saw was gone. Draven shook his head and looked again, still nothing. The clouds were pressing more burdensome overhead. It almost looked like a storm was coming in again. Strange, Draven thought. It was so peaceful and sunny just a moment ago. As he watched the clouds as they rolled in, it almost looked unnatural. Fast and controlled as they moved in and darkened the area. The wind had only increased a little, but hardly enough to move the clouds in such a way.

The others were gazing around the grounds but had noticed the clouds as well. Draven looked over at them then back up. The others didn't seem as concerned about the weather and just made their way slowly inside. Before joining them, Draven looked again up at the tower, and then he saw it. A swirl of bats and smoke whipped around the tower and then back into it. The figure was there for a moment and then gone again.

Draven ran inside, rushing past the others so fast that

they protested his abrupt rudeness. Paying them no mind, Draven rushed inside and up the stairs. He rushed the door that he noticed was closed at the top of the stairs when he came out for breakfast earlier that morning.

As he reached the door, he found it was locked. "Blast it," Draven said under his breath. He calmed a bit as he stepped back and looked up and around the door as if he was looking for something to open the door. The others had now caught up to him on the stairs and questioned him about his behavior.

Draven explained what he saw and that he was concerned. "There's probably a family of bats in that tower, considering that it's open the way it is. The smoke was probably a trick of the eyes," said the Duke, who immediately dismissed the worry.

The ladies agreed with the Duke, and the group was about to depart when the butler came up the stairs to greet them. "The master is still in retreat in his quarters," he said smoothly as he reached the top step. Charlie stood still and tall in front of the group; his hands were behind his back held casually as he stood. "I would appreciate if you wouldn't traipse around so haphazardly," he finished. His expression never changed. It was only after a moment of silence that he turned and walked back down the stairs.

Draven and the others murmured amongst themselves quietly. They continued their disagreements about the recent events, but Draven was unmoved. He knew something wasn't right about the way that the bats and smoke moved and how it matched his dream. He didn't have a logical answer yet, but he needed to keep looking.

After several minutes of bickering, the ladies decided to return to the garden out back. The Duke said that he would be in the library until Lord Bastien called for him. This left Draven to continue his search on his own for now. *I shouldn't see Lord Bastien empty-handed if I can help it,* he thought. If the Lord was correct, and something was trying to kill him, whether it be dreams or real, then perhaps something in the house would give him a clue to what it could be. Draven decided to search the other bedrooms first since the others had gone elsewhere.

After checking the first two rooms, he found nothing unusual. They were, in fact, the same room. As Draven entered the Duke's room nearest his own, he stopped short when he entered, realizing that it wasn't just the room's layout that matched. It was the room! Everything in each of the bedrooms was more than just identical. It was a mirror image. The chairs were in the exact same spot in each one. The candles were the same height with the same amount of wax that had melted the same way. The only difference was the clothes. However, upon further inspection, all the clothes were placed in the same way in every room.

How is this possible? Draven thought to himself. *How could we all have moved the same way and placed everything in the same spot?* Draven continued to think about his as he approached the windows in the Duke's room. Glancing out, he noticed the garden towards the back and how it wrapped around the house on this side. He had noticed it from the outside, but it was nice to see the overview from above in relation to the rooms in the house.

Looking to his left, he could see some of the stables off to the side towards the front of the house. His view was partially blocked from the outside of the tower that ran down the front corner of the Manor. There were no windows in the tower, which Draven thought was strange. He hoped he would get a chance to look in the tower when Lord Bastien was available. He was eager to see the top where he saw the smoke and bats from earlier.

Draven spent the rest of the morning casually waking the house. He paused briefly to view the pictures on the walls, some scenic, others were portraits. Whether they were relatives or just noble figures, Draven didn't know. Draven entered the ballroom and began looking around. Here, he noticed the craftsmanship of the pillars and windows that decorated the room. Two massive chandeliers hung on the ceiling with crystal jewels strung across them. The light from the windows danced around the room as it reflected off them.

More paintings were hung in here, and Draven noticed that one of these seemed different. More lifelike. At first glance, it appeared just like the other oil paintings in the Manor, but the closer he got to it to examine, the more accurate it became. It was a painting of Lord Bastien himself, but so real that one would've thought that he was just standing there. Draven wondered when the painting was done and who painted it, as it was highly accurate and current to Lord Bastien's features.

The eyes followed Draven as he moved back and forth, looking at the portrait from different directions. He stopped after a few times and just continued to stare into the picture. Suddenly, the colors began to change, becoming more apparent. The face of Lord Bastien began to move slowly, turning his head to face Draven more directly. Draven stumbled back a step as he continued to gaze into the picture as it moved. Lord Bastien's image cleared to the point that it looked like Draven was looking at him through a window.

Draven watched as Lord Bastien's image came to life in the portrait. His features changed slightly; his skin became whiter, his cheeks became more sunken in, and his eyes turned a slight shade of yellow. His teeth were pure white, with the canines slightly longer than the rest. Draven's nerves got tense as he watched it unfold. Finally, Lord Bastien leaned forward, almost protruding from the picture frame. He paused. Then spoke, "Only three remain." His voice sounded hollow and ghostly.

Crack! Boom! Thunder sounded loud outside overhead. Draven snapped out his thoughts. He was panting heavily and quickly scanned the room and looked back at the picture of Lord Bastien. Everything had returned to normal. Lord Bastien's image was merely that, an oil-painted image on the canvas. Did I dream it? Was it real? Draven's thoughts took over as he continued to try and calm himself from what had just happened.

"Draven!" Draven almost jumped in his skin as the voice echoed loudly in the house.

"Draven!" the voice echoed again. Draven whirled around to see where it came from. It sounded like Miss Anne, but he wasn't sure.

"Here!" Draven called back as he walked back through the ballroom into the entryway. As he reached the staircase, he met Miss Anne, who was frozen stiff as she looked up the stairs. "What's going on?" he asked urgently. Miss Anne didn't answer, merely pointed up the staircase. Draven followed her finger, but nothing was there, so he headed up to investigate.

As he reached the top, he saw Lady Elizabeth standing in the hallway outside the Duke's room. Draven asked if she was all right, and in her usual proper manner, she insisted she was okay.

    Draven knew better, her hands couldn't stop shaking, and her voice cracked when she spoke. "The Duke," she finally said clearly as she pointed in his room. "I was coming to check up on him as he stated he didn't feel well and wanted to rest. Something he ate, he thought it was."

    Draven slowly entered the room. The shattered pieces of the tea set were strewn about the floor. No doubt they were bringing him tea and brought the ladies up to see the Duke in his room. He paused in the doorway to look around the room before entering. Whatever scared the ladies enough to drop the dishes should be visible from this viewpoint.

    Then he saw Draven's gaze stop short when it reached the bed. There was the Duke, lying there stiff as a board. His left hand was missing. Only broken pieces of the forearm remained visible through the bottom of his sleeve. His right hand was gripping his left arm below the break. Blood had soaked his clothes and the bed around him. As Draven approached, he noticed the blood was already dried up. He glanced over and saw the windows were closed, so there wasn't any steady airflow. Draven looked back at the rigid body of the Duke. His skin looked utterly dried out.

    Draven would've guessed that the Duke was dead for weeks, and the body just dried up at this initial inspection. All his skin was only slightly discolored but sunken in, and his muscle density was significantly less. Draven carefully poked at the Duke's body with a pencil he pulled from his coat pocket. Completely rigid, no elasticity or moisture could be seen or revealed in the body. Draven exhaled heavily as he stood back up and continued to think as he looked up and down the scene. Miss Anne had joined the Lady Elizabeth in the doorway at this time. Both ladies seemed relatively calmer than before.

"So, what do we do?" the Lady Elizabeth asked as Draven made his way back to them in their direction.

"Find the butler," Draven said firmly. He stepped quickly between the girls and exited the room. "Stay here and keep watch," he said as he walked down the hallway to the stairs. The ladies looked at each other in slight disgust, glancing back in the room at the Duke, then slowly stepping back into the hallway.

"Charlie!" Draven called from the staircase as he got to the main floor. His voice echoed loudly in the entry, and for a moment, he felt bad that his voice might wake Lord Bastien. He quickly dismissed this thought as the death of the Duke was more important at the moment. "Charlie!" he called again, louder this time.

Chapter 5

"Charlie!" Draven called again. He had remained near the front door, which was central to the house, so from here, he figured his voice would carry the easiest covering the most distance.

"Yes, sir," came a voice from behind him. Draven about jumped out of his skin and turned around quickly to see the butler standing in the doorway of the front door. The door was closed behind him, and Draven wondered how he got in without him noticing.

Draven quickly shook this thought and said, "The Duke is dead in his room." Charlie's expression didn't change much upon hearing this news. Draven waited for a moment to see what kind of reaction or response the butler might give him. Charlie didn't move. His face remained emotionless. Draven grew tense and finally snapped, "Well?"

"Lord Bastien is awake now and will address you shortly," Charlie said in a smooth unchanging tone.

Draven scoffed loudly and turned abruptly to go back upstairs. As he returned to the room, the ladies had calmed down and were murmuring. Draven couldn't hear enough of the conversation to know what the topic was exactly. However, based on their tones and concern, it seemed they were speculating possible theories about what happened or what was going to happen next.

As Draven approached them, Miss Anne was the first to

notice and quickly asked, "What's the word?" Her tone was smooth, but Draven could tell that the question was full of more fear than she cared to show.

Draven paused a moment before answering. He stared into the room, the Duke's body was still dried upon his bed, and the clouds grew darker out the windows. Thunder boomed outside. It was getting louder as Draven walked through the room to the window. The ladies walked behind him as they waited for his response. "Well?" the Lady Elizabeth interjected, breaking Draven's thoughts.

Draven turned away from the window to face them. "Lord Bastien will be available soon." The girls' expressions relaxed a little. Draven didn't show any concern or relief. His thoughts were too focused on the connection between what Lord Bastien said the evening prior and his dream and now the death of the Duke.

Boom! Draven turned his head quickly over his shoulder to look outside again. No rain again, just thunder and clouds. It was early afternoon, but it almost felt like evening due to the cloud cover darkening. Strange, Draven thought. "When the Lord arrives, we will discuss this further," he said, turning back to the ladies. "Charlie seemed less than surprised or concerned when I mentioned it to him."

"Humph," the Lady Elizabeth snorted. "Well, I'll be sure to give them both a piece of my mind about this matter." She made her way back to the door and looked down the hall as if she was waiting for someone to meet her. Draven and Miss Anne glanced at each other with a sign of annoyance and concern. Both facial expressions were understood by the other. After a moment, they joined Elizabeth at the doorway.

Miss Anne was about to suggest that someone find the

Lord or Charlie and make them come up here, but as she was about to speak, a chill ran through the trio. Draven turned and looked around quickly, there was no wind or moving air in the house, but the temperature dropped significantly. The ladies moved in closer to each other as the cold got stronger.

Draven ran to the stairs and called for Charlie and Lord Bastien. No response. He made his way back to the Duke's room. The ladies had stepped inside the room again, attempting to get warmer. As Draven met them, it suddenly stopped. Whatever was making the air cold was almost instantly reversed.

As the warmth returned, the trio again returned to the hallway and then made their way to the staircase. Lord Bastien was already walking up the stairs towards the group. Charlie was close behind. Draven observed them coming up the stairs and noticed they moved in almost perfect harmony together, smooth strides with barely a shift in the upper body as they ascended. Draven and the ladies stepped back a few steps as Lord Bastien reached the top. "Some trouble I hear," the Lord said. The ladies nodded. Draven just stood motionless. He stared at Lord Bastien, looking for some concern or emotion to read. None was found in the Lord as they walked past the group to the Duke's room.

"You said this house was trying to kill you," Draven said sharply as he walked behind Lord Bastien. "And while I believe that there may be something here, I need more information about what you suspect and why." They stopped outside the Duke's room for a moment. The thunder was still pounding outside, Lightning flashes reflected in the windows slightly, the bit of sun was still trying to shine through the cloud cover. It had darkened quite a bit, but it was still more grey and gloomy outside than straight night black.

"Let us deal with this before we answer your inquires," Lord Bastien said, turning his head to face Draven. Draven nodded in acknowledgment and proceeded to follow the Lord into the room. "Wait here," Lord Bastien said firmly. Draven stopped short and the ladies behind him as well. He felt the desire to obey the request again, but not because it was of his own will.

Lord Bastien approached the bed where the Duke's body was and quickly examined it. Draven turned to Charlie, but the butler ignored his gaze and continued to watch the work of Lord Bastien. Draven then turned his eye back into the room. Lord Bastien continued to examine the Duke's body and the surrounding area within the room. After a few moments, he joined the group in the doorway. "Charlie," he said smoothly. "Arrange for the Duke's body to be taken into town. Afterward, we'll take lunch in the main dining hall."

"Very good, sir," Charlie replied and bowed his head slightly.

Turning to the others, Lord Bastien asked them to remain calm and that they should go outside for some fresh air before lunch. Again, Draven and the others felt compelled to follow Lord Bastien's instructions. However, Draven still noticed that while he wanted to do what he was told, he could feel himself resisting the request in the back of his mind, a futile attempt, though. The trio walked outside through the back as they had before earlier that morning. Lord Bastien remained inside with Charlie to help remove the Duke's rigid corpse.

Thunder was still sounding in the sky, and the cloud cover was very thick. The air was chilly, but the wind was fair, so it was comfortable to be outside other than the seeming inevitability of rain. The ladies had taken to strolling around the garden area while Draven sat on the bench and stared at the Manor. His eyes roamed the sides of the house that he could see, scanning every inch carefully. The vines covered much of the back side, encroaching on the sides slightly in places. Draven walked a bit now to get a better view of the side of the Manor with the tower that he noticed earlier. Nothing of note was seen.

    Draven sat at the fountain. The water was clear and reflected everything. Draven stared at his reflection in the water as he thought about the events happening. He zoned out for a moment. Then, suddenly, a ripple showed in the water. Then another. Soon, several ripples in the water moved through it, distorting the image of the scene reflected there.

    Draven snapped out of his thoughts as he noticed that the reflection had changed. The background became dark and distorted, smoke or bats he couldn't tell as it looked the same. He stood for a moment more as he watched as his reflection became that of Lord Bastien, but he was different here. The reflection showed Lord Bastien's skin whiter than Draven had noticed in person. His cheeks were sunken in a bit, and then he spoke with a smooth and clear voice. "Only two remain." The reflection smiled and laughed with an evil maniacal laugh. Draven couldn't move. Try as he might, he was frozen in place.

    Two fangs became visible in Lord Bastien's mouth where the canine teeth would be as he continued to laugh. Draven felt his body grow weak…

    Splash! Draven snapped back to reality as he realized that he had fallen into the fountain. After a few minutes of splashing frantically, he managed to get up and step out back on dry land. Not a moment later, an ear-piercing scream flooded the area. The girls, Draven thought to himself. Without hesitation, he ran forward toward where the ladies had been walking last he saw.

As he got to the scene, he saw the Lady Elizabeth half-frozen in terror and ghostly white. Draven, still dripping wet, followed her gaze until he saw it. The rotten form of the young Miss Anne laying in the flowerbed. Draven paused a moment to take in the scene, then carefully approached the body.

Miss Anne looked half decayed. Rotting flesh and tissue were all that remained. Holes in her body from where bugs had begun eating away at her flesh. Draven slowly stood back up and faced Lady Elizabeth. She was calmer now as the fear and shock wore off. "Just like the dream," Draven said softly. Elizabeth nodded quickly in agreement as she leaned in to rest her head on Draven's shoulder. Whatever smug attitude she had had before, she was quickly humbled by the events of the last two days.

"But how can her body get like that so quickly?" Elizabeth said as she gently pushed away from Draven's embrace. Draven shook his head as he turned back to face Miss Anne's body. "I only turned my back for a few moments when this happened."

"You know the answer, as well do I," he said after a brief pause. "This house." Draven then led Lady Elizabeth away from the scene to help her mental state and get some distance between them and the body. Draven began discussing with the Lady how Lord Bastien had said the house was trying to kill him, but he hadn't been touched yet. Furthermore, both Lord Bastien and Charlie seem unfazed by what had happened so far.

"Do you think others have tried before, and the house killed them too?" Lady Elizabeth asked.

"I'm not sure," Draven replied. "But I'm becoming less convinced about Lord Bastien's need for safety and more concerned about ours."

"So, what do we do?"

"Lord Bastien should be coming to fetch us soon, and then we'll tell him about Miss Anne," Draven said plainly. He didn't bother to tell her about Lord Bastien's portrait or the reflection in the water. No need to add fuel to her concern about the situation already. The sky turned darker, Draven and Elizabeth didn't stray too far for fear that Miss Anne's body would disappear on them.

Draven stayed deep in thought; he waited. He was trying to put all the pieces together of the events of the last two days. The dream, the portrait, the reflection in the pool, the weather, the smoke around the tower, the Duke's death, and now Miss Anne's; the chill in the house, the darkness, the fangs; Draven had some ideas. A few possibilities came to mind, none of them logical. However, they were the only ones that made sense. If they were to get out alive, they would have to move quickly to solve this mystery.

Chapter 6

It was longer than they wanted to wait for Lord Bastien to come outside to meet them. Additionally, he seemed unaffected by the additional death. In fact, Lord Bastien's demeanor was so upbeat and chipper considering the horror that was taking place, that Draven almost thought that the Lord was enjoying this.

"Is everything all right?" Lord Bastien asked as he approached. Lady Elizabeth shot him a piercing glance. Lord Bastien remained unfazed. Draven had to do a double-take as Lord Bastien got closer, since seeing the Lord in the Duke's room, his skin looked fairer, almost younger with his hair looking darker and fuller as well as more minor pauses in his steps.

Draven stepped to the side to reveal Miss Anne's body still lying in the dirt. Draven noticed that she looked even more decomposed than she did when he discovered her moments before.

As Lord Bastien walked closer, Draven could've sworn that the features in Lord Bastien's face changed, not much, but just enough. As he walked closer to Miss Anne's body, it seemed that Lord Bastien was getting younger. Draven shook the thought. Even of the crazy ideas and plausible options that Draven had been thinking of, this one seemed even more ridiculous.

However, as Lord Bastien knelt near Miss Anne's corpse,

Draven and Lady Elizabeth noticed that her body was almost decomposing faster into the ground. The couple watched as the Lord stood still, looking at the remnants of Miss Anne poking through the dirt. "It's time to go inside," said Lord Bastien. He didn't move naught but his head as he spoke, only enough to glance over his shoulder at Draven and the Lady standing behind him.

Draven turned to walk inside, feeling a sense of obedience again that he wanted yet, didn't want. The clouds were still dark overhead. Draven couldn't tell what time it was by the sky since the sunlight could barely reflect through. The Lady Elizabeth was on his left, clinging to his arm. They walked up the garden steps and into the house. She had a blank stare on her face, shock and horror most likely. Draven figured that she was probably running through similar scenarios about what was going on here. Draven didn't show it as much, and she did, but he was just as scared.

Once they entered the library, the butler greeted them, and both Draven and the Lady felt more at ease with the fire burning warm and tea being served. "Is everything going well?" Charlie asked as he poured the tea and handed it to Lady Elizabeth first. Elizabeth said nothing and only sat and sipped her tea, seemingly lost in thought.

Taking the chance in the silence, Draven ignored Charlie's question as well and asked one of his own, "Have the proper arrangements been made for the Duke?" The butler only nodded gently as he poured the tea that would be Draven's. "And now for Miss Anne?" Draven asked further, hoping to get a more definitive answer about what was going on.

Charlie brought Draven his tea and said nothing at first. "Tragic loss," he muttered softly. It was so soft that Draven almost missed that it was said.

"Yes, it is," Draven agreed firmly. "And quite frankly, I'm of the mind to leave these heinous acts to you and your master," he stated as he got up. Then, turning to her, said, "We're leaving."

"You'll do no such thing," a voice echoed from the entrance of the room. Draven turned to see Lord Bastien standing there. But, this time, Draven was sure that he looked younger now. His features were distinctly changed from the evening before now. Lord Bastien went from a man that looked almost eighty, with greying hair and a frail figure to a man of full stature with the complexion of a thirty-year-old.

Draven stood facing Lord Bastien as he walked forward. Lady Elizabeth sat up more alert and present as the air grew tense between Draven and Lord Bastien. "Sit down," the Lord said firmly. Draven's legs didn't even hesitate, much to his own surprise, as he collapsed on the chair he was standing in front of. Draven glanced over at Lady Elizabeth with slight shock and confusion. Elizabeth only met his gaze with a fear-filled face of her own.

"Very little has been done to solve my puzzle," Lord Bastien began to say. He waved a hand at Charlie, and the butler took that cue to leave. "And instead, gotten two of your group killed in the process," he finished.

"Hard to determine what is killing you since you get younger as we die," Draven said defiantly. He sat because he had to but crossed his arms and posed firm in his seat, facing Lord Bastien. Lord Bastien only glanced at Draven before turning to give his full attention to Lady Elizabeth.

"And you, my dear?" Lord Bastien asked calmly. He seated himself next to her comfortably. Only Elizabeth's eyes moved to meet the Lord's gaze upon her. She said nothing and didn't move more than that. Lord Bastien put his arm around Lady Elizabeth's shoulders and looked back at Draven and smiled. "Theories?" he asked questioningly, in almost a rhetorical tone.

"Some possibilities, perhaps," Draven answered. He didn't want to give away too much too soon. That's when Draven saw it, or didn't see it, rather. The reflection on the silver part of the teacup showed Lady Elizabeth sitting there, but no Lord Bastien. Draven's mind flew in an instant. He recalled that in the layout of each bedroom upstairs, no mirrors were present. He quickly remembered the front hall, and the kitchen, also no mirrors. He glanced again at the teacup in front of him and double-checked his eyesight. It was the same, the reflection of Lady Elizabeth without Lord Bastien beside her.

Lord Bastien could tell that Draven was thinking. His smile grew more as he watched Draven. His eyes grew intense as time slowed for the Lord. He waited patiently for Draven to put the pieces together. Then finally, after what seemed like an eternity for Lord Bastien, Draven shifted his focus back to the present.

To Draven, this thought passed in mere seconds. He hardly noticed his facial features changing as he thought. As his gaze focused on Lord Bastien again, Draven saw the smile; this was the missing piece. Lord Bastien's teeth, the canines were much longer than they should be. "Vampire," Draven said to himself. Lord Bastien's smile only got more intense. Tales and scary stories were all Draven had ever considered when it came to the existence of vampires and other such monsters. And, as much as he tried to explain away the situation, Draven could not deny it any longer and therefore had to admit that he was, in fact, face to face with a vampire.

At this acknowledgment, Lady Elizabeth pulled away from Lord Bastien and got up quickly to leave. Lord Bastien let her get a few steps away before acting. With lightning speed, Lord Bastien grabbed the plate that held the teapot and accessories, spilling everything. Draven tensed in his chair as it unfolded before him. Lord Bastien hurled the disk at Lady Elizabeth like a metal Frisbee with super speed and a fluid motion.

Draven only saw the aftermath. He turned to look at the sound of the tray slashing into the wall on the far side of the room. Lady Elizabeth stood motionless. Draven saw the tray stuck in the wall on the other side of her. Lord Bastien was standing to Draven's left, calm and casual. Lady Elizabeth slowly turned around to face the gentlemen. Draven watched as a trickle of blood started to show up on her neck. Her face was fixed in a state of shock as she slowly reached up and put her hands on each side of her head. The blood coming from the line across her neck started to pour out faster through the cut; as this happened, Lady Elizabeth pulled her head off her shoulders, and it separated smoothly on the line that was already bleeding.

As she brought her head down to her side, her body collapsed. As it hit the floor, that was Draven's cue to leave. He jumped up, throwing his teacup at Lord Bastien, and darted towards the door to the library. Jumping over the body of Lady Elizabeth, Draven got to the entrance and darted into the hall. Echoes of Lord Bastien laughing could be heard coming from the library or the upstairs; Draven couldn't tell and didn't care as he headed towards the front door.

In a blur, Lord Bastien moved past Draven and stood in the doorway, blocking the exit. "Leaving so soon?" he asked mockingly. "We still haven't solved the mystery of this house." Draven paused only long enough to collect his thoughts before turning on his heel and heading upstairs.

Lord Bastien touched the doorframe and called after Draven as he ascended the steps, "You have no chance here, Draven. This house is my power." Draven turned to glance back and saw Lord Bastien disappear into smoke.

Reaching the balcony at the top of the stairs, Draven quickly determined his plan: run, hide, escape. The air grew cold again, and Draven didn't need to look up to know that the darkness was filling the ceiling again, just like his dream. The wind picked up, though no windows were open. Smoke and bats suddenly filled the hall. Draven fell to the floor in terror. Only one remains! The voice echoed in his head, but it wasn't his. Panic started to sink in as he crawled across the floor.

The red eyes appeared through the smoke above Draven as he went. The smoke turned to bats again and flew around him, hitting him and biting him as they did. Only one remains! The voice echoed in his head again. Draven shook it off to think. The eyes followed him. The red glow was ever pressing on his back as he crawled around the floor. Then, suddenly, an idea popped into Draven's mind. The tower.

Quickly Draven turned, and with a new focus, he pushed through the smoke and bats. The closer he got to the door of the tower, the more intense he could feel the darkness grabbing at him. Just like the dream, the bats turned to smoke again, and the darkness reached out at him with finger-like entrails that, when they touched Draven, he shuddered instantly.

Reaching the door, he felt frantically for the handle. The darkness wrapped around his leg, sending a chilling feeling through him as he did. Laughter echoed above him, deep and malicious. A heaviness pressed in on Draven's mind as he attempted to open to door. The door handle turned, but the door refused to give. Draven threw all his weight into it. As he did, the door swung open freely, and Draven landed hard on the floor.

Draven got up enough to kick the door shut. As it clicked closed, he raced for the stairs. The stone steps spiraled up around the outer edge of the tower. The tower diameter was wide, so the ascent felt long and slow as he climbed. Lord Bastien's laughter could be heard echoing below him, and Draven began to wonder if he was headed for a trap.

Reaching the first room, Draven climbed up onto the central part of the floor. The steps had just wrapped around the outer wall and came up through the floor of the room he was now in. Across the way, Draven could see another set of stairs continuing in the same fashion headed up further to another floor above him. That must lead to the top floor, he thought to himself.

The current room had a red-colored rug that reached the walls on all sides. A lone window barely big enough to get his head through, not that it mattered, the thick glass and bars would prevent anyone short of a mouse from getting through. The walls were bare, and there was no furniture, except for a lone decorative wooden coffin laying in the center of the room.

Draven thought quickly on how he would obtain some means of either escape or Lord Bastien's defeat. Suddenly, a chill went up Draven's spine. He whirled around to see the darkness creeping up the stairs toward him. Only one remains. Lord Bastien's voice echoed in his head again. Draven dropped to one knee and grabbed at his head in pain. You cannot escape. This is my power. Each time the voice spoke, Draven's head hurt with incredible pain.

The coffin, Draven thought to himself, in the moment of clarity he got. His head was still reeling from the pain of Bastien's voice inside. Draven got up slowly and grabbed the coffin. The darkness was in the room now, forcing its way in, expanding along the walls. Draven held one end of the coffin and pulled towards the stairs on the other side of the room with all his strength. Once he reached them, he looked up at the darkness closing in. The red eyes appeared within it. They glowed with a new fervor. Draven suddenly felt a stinging sensation as the eyes penetrated to his very core.

Pausing only for a moment to recompose himself, Draven continued to haul the coffin around the circular steps and up to the top of the tower. He didn't have to go far until he reached the door. It was flat above him and opened up and folded over on the stone floor of the open tower. The wind was blowing hard up here as Draven looked around to see what he could. Grey clouds were thick and heavy. Thunder crashed loudly above him. The tower floor was completely open, with stone columns decoratively spaced around the edge to hold up the roof. Within the roof rafters, Draven saw bats. So many they covered the inside of the top above him.

Quickly pulling the coffin to the edge of the tower, he wasn't even sure if this would work. But it was his best option given the circumstance as Draven braced against a column to steady himself while he started to slide the coffin off the edge.

The bats suddenly started shrieking above him. He glanced up to see them in a frenzy then, flying around in a swirled pattern above him going all over. Then suddenly, they all headed towards the trap door that Draven had just come up through.

Darkness poured up through the door, and the bats flew into it with startling speed. As they met the darkness, the smoke and bats took the form of Lord Bastien. He smiled menacingly as he walked towards Draven. "Only one remains," he said smoothly. Draven swallowed hard as he backed to the edge.

Summoning his courage, Draven drew a quick deep breath and yanked the coffin off the edge of the tower. "Nooo!" Lord Bastien shrieked as he lurched forward. Draven only smiled as he stood upright and faced Lord Bastien for the last time. Lord Bastien reached out to grab Draven, but it was too late. Draven was already falling, sacrificing himself. For Draven, time began to slow slightly. Looking up, he could see Lord Bastien at the edge of the tower looking down at him. His face was filled with anger, and his body barely held its form as the smoke and bats started to peel out of him. Turning towards the ground, Draven saw the coffin burst into dozens of pieces as it impacted on the ground. At the last second, he looked back up to see Lord Bastien's form dissipate into just smoke and bats that swirled aimlessly around. Then, it all went black.

Chapter 7

Draven awoke and lurched up in his bed. He was sweating and breathing heavily as he glanced around the room. The outside light was coming in through the windows behind the curtains. Draven started to come to his complete senses. He noticed the room he was in was his bedroom in the Manor. Feeling his body around anxiously as he stepped out of bed, he was trying to verify the reality of the situation.

Once Draven was comfortable, and his mind calmed somewhat, he looked around the room and saw that everything was as it was the night he arrived. After getting dressed, Draven exited the room and was shocked at the sight. The manor was in complete disrepair. Giant cobwebs hung in various places, from the ceiling and around the doors of the other rooms. When he checked the other rooms, the furniture was broken and bedsheets half rotten. There was no sign of anyone having been there in decades.

Quickly Draven checked through each room, and it was the same throughout. Reaching the balcony of the main staircase, the rest of the house was no different. Some of the windows were broken in places; others had a thick layer of dust and dirt stuck to them. Rot had set into the trim and wall in several areas. Reaching the main floor, Draven headed through the library. It was just as destroyed as the rest of the house. Several books were strewn about, and most of the shelves were empty. This was the opposite of the full shelves and warm and welcome atmosphere that he remembered.

Pausing near the couch that other guests had been sitting at, Draven started to think about everything that had happened. The events replayed in his head over and over. He turned to look at the spot that Lady Elizabeth had fallen after her head was cut off. There was no sign of her. The wall where the tray, thrown by Lord Bastien, made contact didn't have any trace of the impact.

Curious about the other deaths, Draven headed through the kitchen and outside to see the garden where Miss Anne met her fate. The backyard looked just as rough as the house, overgrown with weeds and dead leaves covering everything. The fountain was empty and full of dead leaves, scum and moss. Draven headed over to the garden spot, and it too, like the rest, was completely overgrown.

Even if Miss Anne's body were there, buried beneath, he would never know. Glancing back up at the house, Draven could see the extent of the damage and disrepair it was in. The exterior had pieces missing, and the roof looked like it was barely holding together. The wind blew softly, early autumn was here, and the crisp air was a token to that.

Draven entered the manor through the rear kitchen door. Everything was torn apart by rot and decay here as well. Walking through the dining room and back to the main hall, Draven found his coat where the butler had placed it when he arrived, though now, the surrounding area was dirty and falling apart. So much so that as Draven took his coat from the hook, it broke, and the whole wall fixture fell, taking a piece of the wall with it.

Draven stood silent for a moment collecting his thoughts. Is this the dream? Or was the entire event a dream? Surely, he didn't dream up the invitation from Lord Bastien to come here. Draven continued to think as he walked back out into the entryway by the main door. He paused before exiting. A slight chill ran down his spine. Draven turned towards the stairs and the entrance to the tower where he had faced Lord Bastien, or at least, he thought he faced Lord Bastien. Everything was blurring together, and Draven had a hard time splitting dreams from reality and the idea that vampires are real.

Draven dropped his coat by the door and quickly walked upstairs. "The proof is here. I know it," He muttered to himself. Reaching the tower door, he paused again to listen. Nothing but the wind was heard. Satisfied, Draven entered and slowly walked up the circular staircase to the room where the coffin was found. But here, Draven found nothing. The room was completely empty, with no rug nor furniture to be seen. Only cobwebs and dust throughout. Walking up further, Draven reached the tower level and opened the trap door above him to get out.

The wind hit him hard as he stepped up on the tower floor. Here looked the same as he remembered – the open floor and pillars around the outer edge. Looking up, Draven noticed that it was empty in the inner roof that covered him. Walking to the edge, he looked down to see where he had pulled the coffin off and where he, himself, had fallen in an attempt to escape his fate with Lord Bastien.

Draven knelt and peered over the edge. The ground at the bottom looked as it did when Draven was outside earlier, with no trace of the coffin. Feeling more confused, Draven got up and headed back to the trap door to descend the tower and leave the Manor. Draven shut all the doors behind him and did one final brief walkthrough. As he did, he came across the spot where the portrait of Lord Bastien had moved earlier and came alive. However, as with every other trace of the events that just unfolded, this piece was missing too.

More questions just flooded into Draven's mind as he headed to the door. He knew what happened, and he knew what he saw and felt. Grabbing his coat, Draven decided he would inquire about the Duke, Miss Anne and Lady Elizabeth when he finally returned to the city. Those were real people, so there must be some trace of their existence somewhere.

As Draven exited the main door, he jumped in his skin slightly. There, waiting for him at the base of the stairs, was his carriage and driver. Draven walked down towards the carriage as the driver opened the door for him with a comely bow as he did so. "Good morning, sir," he stated casually as he stood back up to greet Draven.

"Good morning," Draven replied quickly. "How did you know to be here?" he asked before entering the carriage.

"Your letter, sir," the man replied. "You stated that you would be ready for pickup promptly at eight o'clock in the morning today."

"How long have you waited for me?"

"I've only just arrived, sir."

"And the time?" Draven asked as he climbed into his seat.

"Eight o'clock." The driver closed the door and stepped up into his seat in front to depart. Draven felt the gentle jolt of the horses as they began to pull away. The front path was just as destroyed as the back of the Manor, with dead leaves and overgrowth all around. The lamp posts that were lit as Draven approached the other night now appeared to be unable to be much more than plain fixtures along the driveway. Some were missing pieces of the glass housing. Others were broken off at the base and lying on the ground nearby.

What was the truth about the Manor? What was the truth about Lord Bastien? Who were the others, and was it perhaps all a dream? Draven thought about these questions and more as he headed home. Replaying the events over and over in his mind didn't clear up any of his memories. Nor was he able to tell what was dream or reality.

The only truth that Draven could tell was that he was dropped off two days ago and picked up now. He was glancing back through the carriage window at the Manor as it sat in the distance. Perhaps he beat the vampire, and this was the reset? Maybe he dreamed the whole thing and had a dream within the dream? But why did he get the letter to arrive in the first place, and what compelled him to be dropped off to investigate?

The rest of the ride home was uneasy as Draven was lost in his thoughts about the whole ordeal. Once he arrived home, Draven found a letter left on his front step. It was unmarked save only Draven's name on the front. Opening the letter, Draven's face went white. Written in the center was only one phrase:

"Only one remains."

– L. B.

Draven then knew that he was, in fact, not dreaming and that everything that happened was real. There was no telling how long the letter had been sitting there or who delivered it since he had been gone most of the morning returning from the manor.

Tense and frightened, Draven walked around his grounds

to clear his head. If Lord Bastien was still alive and a threat, then why was Draven left alive at the manor? How did he survive the fall off the tower? After some time and more thinking, Draven realized that, until a real threat exposed itself, he would continue on and not worry too much about it.

As time went on, Draven thought less and less about the Manor or Lord Bastien. He had given up on trying to locate the other members that were present with him after a few days of no results. Granted, he didn't have much to go on and didn't look far beyond the local area.

The more days that went by, the more Draven felt that he might never get the answers he needed. He thought about trying to tell others and returning to the Manor to see if anything had changed. But he reconsidered this since he knew that no one would believe him. To Draven, the events would always be a mystery, and forever, hidden would be, the secrets of Bastien Manor.

END